DECODING SPONSORSHIP

MAGGIE CHAN JONES

Tenshey Publishing

Copyright © 2021

Maggie Chan Jones

Decoding Sponsorship: The Secret Strategy to Accelerate Your Career and Launch Into Leadership

ISBN 978-1-7376557-2-5 Paperback

ISBN 978-1-7376557-0-1 Ebook

ISBN 978-1-7376557-1-8 iBook

CONTENTS

*TO MY GRANDMOTHER, MY MOM, AUNT MEI WAH,
AND AUNT IMY*

for showing me what strong women look like

*TO MY HUSBAND JP AND OUR FOUR-LEGGED KID
CHARLIE*

for our life adventures together

TO MY GODCHILDREN AVERY AND PAXTON

for your inspiration to make the world better

INTRODUCTION

"OK. I'll go."

Those three words changed the course of my life forever. They no doubt broke my mom's heart while simultaneously filling it with hope.

It was my mom who taught me to make difficult decisions. It was my mom who instilled in me the value of a good education. And it was my mom who selflessly fought to ensure I had more opportunities and choices in my life than she had had in hers.

My mom, Mei, loved learning, loved studying, and she loved going to school. But that all came to an abrupt end when she was just 12 years old.

It was 1962. Officially you needed to be at least 16 years old to work in a factory. But at that time in Hong Kong, it was common practice for kids as young as my Mom to get a fake ID and go to work. "I felt so sad I could not go to school," I remember my mom telling me. She knew education was the key to a better life. Yet, as the second oldest of five children, it was her duty to drop out of school and begin working to support the family, just like her older sister before her.

So at an age when most American children are just beginning junior high, my mom packed lunch and headed to a factory to ensure there would be lunches to pack for her three younger siblings.

This was nothing extraordinary in a family-first culture of Hong Kong in the sixties. It was simply her turn, her duty, and her responsibility to the family.

My mom was part of the post WWII baby boom generation. It was a time when families were large, wages were small, and many children worked in the factories. Abundant cheap labor has been cited by historians as one of the main reasons for Hong Kong's economic comeback. The country was devastated at the end of the war. But during the fifties and sixties, a large number of small factories began producing everything from textiles and clothing to plastics and electronics. And so it was that my mother started soldering motherboards in an electronics factory when she was only 12 years old.

Throughout the world, the 1960s proved to be a decade of great change. Hong Kong was no exception. It was a decade of tremendous growth. Fifty percent of the population was under the age of 25. The Beatles captivated, workers protested, and cultural change was in the air.

Still it was a patriarchal society. Just as it was a common place for children to work in factories, there was nothing out of the ordinary for a man to take on multiple wives. That is until 1971, when Hong Kong made polygamy illegal. It was one of the big changes to come out of the decade of change. So, when my mother married in 1972, she wasn't expecting to share her husband with anyone. But things don't always work out the way we expect.

The promising young investor that my mother married found himself out of luck, out of money, and out of work when the oil embargo hit and the stock market crashed in 1973. The impact was devastating in Hong Kong, forcing untold numbers into extreme poverty.

With no jobs to be found, my Dad left my mom and traveled to New York City where he waited tables in a Chinatown restaurant. That was in May of 1974, six months before I was born.

My mom's strength has always been a source of inspiration to me. She taught me to believe in myself and instilled an idea that has guided me throughout my career. It is the profound belief that I can reach for any opportunity I want; that there are no limitations, only realities that can be prepared for and responded to.

The reality for my mom in 1974 was harsh. She was a twenty-four-year-old factory worker with an infant and an absentee husband. We lived with my grandmother, my two aunts, and later my younger cousin who was like a sister. My mom was a key supporter of our family. I can only imagine how difficult it must have been.

As you may have figured out, my mom is a very strong and pragmatic woman. When she didn't hear from my dad and suspected that things weren't right, she responded to her reality by seeking the truth. In 1977, when I was just three years old, my mom left me in the care of my grandmother and headed to New York. When she found my dad, she discovered another harsh reality. In America, he had another wife, another family, and another kid on the way.

After a few agonizing months, her response was to get a divorce.

Still she kept in touch with my father. Often over the phone, seeking child support. When he would return to Hong Kong to visit his mom, she was sure to provide him with updates about me. When I developed asthma and needed expensive medication or trips to the ER, she made sure he knew it was his responsibility to pay.

It wasn't until I was seven years old that I finally met my dad. My mom took me to a café and there he was. I don't remember much about that day. To me, it was like meeting a distant uncle or one of those relatives who live far away that you see only once every few years.

I didn't know him. I didn't have a relationship with him. And even though I was envious of my cousins and friends who had both parents, I didn't really miss having a dad. Mostly because my mom filled that role. She went to work every day and provided for the family. My grandmother was like my mom in the traditional sense. My grandmother cooked dinners and was there every day to drop me off and pick me up from school. My aunts and cousins were there too. We were a big happy family in an apartment crowded with love.

We, all six of us, lived in a tiny apartment in a high-rise building, about 400 square feet. Though we had food on the table and a roof over our heads, by anyone's measure, we were just getting by. Even though I didn't miss my dad, I always felt that I was inferior because I didn't have the things that other kids had, like a Barbie doll, a bike, or two parents. My mom wanted desperately for me to have a better life and she instilled in me the idea that education was the key.

In Hong Kong in the eighties, being a university student marked you as a future member of the elite. Upon graduation, there would be numerous job offers and the promise of career advancement. My mom knew this. Being a realist, she also knew I didn't have the kind of grades it would take to get in. In 1988 there were only three universities in Hong Kong. Only kids in the top 2% of the class academically had any chance of going to college. While I was a good student, I was far from the top 2%.

Remember, my mom doesn't believe in limitations. She's always taught me to look for opportunity and she was always on the lookout herself. When she was in New York in 1977 searching for my father, she saw a potential opportunity in the American education system. She didn't know what that opportunity would be or how it would manifest. She just thought that if I could finish high school in Hong Kong, I could go to a university in America.

In Hong Kong at that time, the first nine years of education were free. After that, you'd have to pay tuition. For years, my mom had been negotiating with my dad, trying to convince him that he should live up to his fatherly responsibility and provide support so that I could continue my education beyond 9th grade. She believed that the best thing was for me to go to school in the United States.

My beloved grandmother did not like the idea. In fact, she repeatedly challenged my mom, saying it would be much easier for me to stay in Hong Kong. She was brought up in the traditional way. How she was raised, a woman should, if she's lucky that is, get married early, have kids and raise a family. That's how she was brought up. She viewed it as the easier path. She knew that if I were to stay in Hong Kong, I would have a loving family there for support.

I didn't know it at the time, but my mom and grandmother argued frequently about this. Both wanted what was best for me. So at the age of fourteen, I was presented with a choice and told that the decision was all mine.

"Maggie, your dad has finally agreed to let you live with him so you can study in the U.S." My mom told me one night during dinner. "Do you want to go?"

The question was no surprise. My mom and I had spoken many times about the importance of a good education and I had overheard her conversations on the phone with my dad.

"Your dad has agreed to let you study in the U.S. and live with him and his family," she continued. "If you go, you'll be able to go to college, if you don't and you stay in Hong Kong, at most you will finish high school and get a job. I really think this is a great opportunity for you. But this is your decision. So you tell me, what do you want to do? Do you want to go? Or do you want to stay?"

At the time, I didn't say anything. I nodded to let her know I had heard and understood what she'd said. But I didn't respond just then. There was so much going through my mind. I didn't know my dad. I didn't know his family. And the fact that he had never even come to see me until I was seven years old, weighed heavily on my mind.

So did the phone conversations I overheard. They were calls in which my mom pleaded with my dad for child support. I remember thinking, I don't ever want to be in that situation. I knew at a young age that I wanted to be independent. To me, that meant I needed to do my best to get a good education. Even though I wasn't looking forward to leaving my family, I knew that education would be the key to my independence.

As I weighed the decision to stay in Hong Kong with my loving family or move half a world away to live with some people I barely knew, a few more of my mom's words ran through my mind.

"Maggie, if you do go and you don't like it" she said, "I'll buy you a plane ticket and you can come home."

Having that safety net made all the difference. It made me feel prepared. Prepared for what might happen in the worst-case scenario. Looking back, I can see how selfless my mother's actions had been. I wanted to go to college. This was my chance. It was a "take it or leave it" kind of thing. I knew I would regret not taking it and I knew I had a safety net, my mom's offer of the plane ticket home. That gave me the confidence I needed to face the unknown.

"OK. I'll go," the three words I told my mother that fateful day in 1988 are three words I've repeated to myself, every time I moved or changed jobs in the years and decades that followed. Three words that represent courage and confidence, risk, reward, and possibilities.

I am glad that my mother had the wisdom and foresight to let it be my decision. As an adult, I often think of the lessons I learned as a young girl in Hong Kong, surrounded by strong women in my family – my grandmother, my mom, and my aunts. I grew up believing I had no limitations, that I could reach for any opportunity if I wanted it badly enough. I was also taught that while I can't control reality, I can prepare for what might happen. And I can respond with hard work, determination, and focus.

These lessons, ingrained since childhood by my mother in Hong Kong, have carried me throughout my personal and professional life. Decades later, as an executive and an advocate for women and people of color in the workplace, I still very much believe, "where there's a will, there's a way."

RISK TAKING AND DECISION MAKING

As I look back on my years as an executive in corporate America, and in my practice at Tenshey, I see many women who struggle with risk taking and decision making - struggles that I faced many times in my life. For me, there was lots of trial and error, however, whenever I could, I tried to learn from others before me.

Taking risks is nerve-racking, but the potential payoff can be huge if you have a plan. In some scenarios, the status quo is so painful, that inaction is not an option. Risk taking is an important part of growth and success, but it's not easy. The key to mitigate those risks is to identify a solution and gain support (if needed) for each element that scares you in making such decisions – just like my decision to leave Hong Kong for New York.

Over the years, there are three things that I have learned to do that helped me achieve my goals.

#1 Take risks

The first thing I learned was to resist the urge to overthink. I've seen women from college graduates to executives talking themselves out of advancements and opportunities without ever even giving it a try. If the opportunity is what you want, just go for it. Put your hat in the ring. Don't think twice. Of course, there's the possibility of being rejected or failing, but what's the worst that can happen? As my mom taught me, you can prepare; if you fail, you will learn a valuable lesson, but if you succeed, the payoff could be huge.

#2 Prepare

The second thing I learned was the importance of preparation. To build confidence, consider having a plan B (or even a plan C). When I was fourteen, my plan B was that plane ticket home. Knowing that gave me the confidence to move forward and go after what I really wanted; a college education in the United States.

When I was climbing the ladder in corporate America, I prepared for important meetings relentlessly. The more I prepared, the more confident I felt. The more confident I felt, the more I embraced the unknown. Not to sound cliche here, but confidence is the key to success, and nothing will build your confidence than preparation and planning.

#3 Focus

The third thing I learned is the power of focus to see your decisions through. For me, having a "Plan B" builds confidence, but focusing on executing against your goal is what leads to success. There will be obstacles. There will be distractions. There will be challenges. But you have to learn to expect the unexpected. There will be fears and frustrations along the way. But those obstacles can only be overcome if you remain focused on the end goal you want.

As I mentioned previously, I learned mostly from trials and errors, but I also love learning through others' experience and journey. I'm writing this book to share the lessons I learned along the way to reach the C-suite in the tech industry.

I hope you enjoy.

Maggie

CREATE YOUR CAREER NORTH STAR

"Knowing yourself is the beginning of all wisdom."

— ARISTOTLE

In 2014, I found myself on a plane heading back to JFK airport in New York - only this time I wasn't coming from Hong Kong like I was nearly 25 years prior as a teenager, and I was not alone.

The opportunity arose for me to become the global Chief Marketing Officer (CMO) of the world's largest enterprise application software company called SAP. It was literally a dream come true. I remember setting the goal of being the CMO of a tech company when I was a group manager at Microsoft years before that. Never in my dreams had I thought I would become the CMO of a company of this size and scale. I felt that my years of experience and the intentional steps I took in my career molded me into the person that was ready to accept such a massive challenge.

So in 2014 my husband, our four-legged kid (a Miniature Poodle) Charlie, and I packed all of our stuff and moved to

New York. I remember being on the plane coming from Denver, Colorado and thinking to myself "Wow, 25 years ago I was a lone fourteen-year-old girl, also flying into JFK airport - not knowing what my future would hold." I just knew that it was something that I needed to do. Twenty-five years later I climbed the corporate ladder to a top job in the marketing profession in one of the most exciting companies in the tech industry. I was no longer alone and scared because I had my family with me. With the backdrop of the beautiful skyline of NYC, that moment crystalized itself in my memory.

But my ascension to the C-suite was not instant, nor was it without its own set of challenges and twists and turns. Here I was, a teenage girl, leaving my mother and grandmother in Hong Kong and moving to New York to live with my dad, my stepmom and half siblings for the first time. I was stepping into a brand new world, brimming with excitement and a sense of inquisitive nervousness, wondering what my future would hold. As I stepped into the building of my new school, John Bowne High School in Queens NY, I was met with the colossal challenge of trying to communicate with others in English, a language I had learned throughout my school years in Hong Kong, then still a British Colony, but rarely had to speak in it.

I eventually went to Binghamton University in Upstate NY, originally pursuing a finance degree because I was good in math, until I was introduced to marketing by Professor Philip Burger in my Marketing 301 class. I was drawn to the intersection of strategy and storytelling and knew that I wanted to pursue a career in marketing someday. I loved the idea of visualizing solutions through a product, in my case tech products, via powerful stories that focus on the customer. I was enamored by the idea of using words and images to elicit emotions that would cause people to take action and buy a product. At the same time, it required strong analytical skills to analyze consumer trends, forecast demand, and adjust plans to meet changing customer needs. In that way, I saw how marketing, when done right, blended left-brain and right-brain disciplines in a way that excited me. I saw how it could humanize cold, lifeless technology and tell a story of how it could change people's lives for the better. Afterall, Bill Gates launched the personal computing revolution in the 1990s by doing just that.

Needless to say, I fell in love with marketing and decided to focus on that. After graduating from Binghamton, I decided to move to Seattle to be closer to my aunt's family in Vancouver B.C. Canada who I am very close with. By then, my mom was able to move to the US to live with me. I was determined to land a job in marketing and sent out more than 100 resumes via "snail" (postal) mail! I had gotten a handful of interviews but it was one rejection after another. It was a grueling process, and at times I felt like giving up.

The questions "Am I good enough?", "Will I ever find a job?", and "What am I doing wrong?" raced through my mind on a daily basis. But I kept pressing on – it's not like I had any other choice.

If you're early in your career and find yourself in the same situation, just know that it *will* get better. Like my mother taught me, you have to focus on what you can control, take risks, and focus on the end goal.

After what felt like a lifetime, I was offered a job as a junior buyer at ADIC, a fast growing data storage company. It wasn't the job I wanted because it wasn't in marketing, but it was a job I needed to pay the bills, so I took it and decided to make the best out of it. "You just have to get your foot in the door, Maggie" I told myself.

Little did I know, I could not have asked for a better way to start my career. I was stepping into a fast growing tech industry that was constantly innovating. That position offered me a strong leadership team, a seasoned manager who taught me so much about negotiations and building successful partnerships, and friendships that lasted a lifetime. With hard work and determination, I was able to transfer internally to a role in marketing at ADIC two and a half years later.

After a few years in Seattle, I found myself drawn to Silicon Valley not only for the vibrant tech scene, but also the warm and sunny weather most of the year. I relocated to Menlo Park, CA to work at Sun Microsystems as a product manager for their carrier-grade systems specifically designed for the booming internet infrastructure industry in early 2000. Those were the days when Sun had coined themselves as "the dot in the dot-com". Business was growing fast and we could barely keep up with the demand for our servers and storage systems. Until the "Internet Bubble" burst, that is.

In 2005, my husband and I decided to move back to Seattle to be closer to our parents. Luckily, I landed a job at Microsoft. Microsoft is where I built the foundation of leadership skills. It's where I formulated my career North Star of being a Chief Marketing Officer at a large software company someday.

From there I rose through the ranks at Microsoft, was pegged as a high-potential leader, and eventually took on a senior executive role at Level 3 Communications before becoming the Global Chief Marketing Officer of SAP.

Throughout my years as an executive, I was fortunate enough to receive industry validation of my work both as a marketing professional and as a leader who's passionate about gender equality. I was named one of the "World's Most Influential CMOs" by Forbes, and received a "Woman of the Decade in Marketing, Branding and Communication" award from the Women's Economic Forum. I was acknowledged for creativity and storytelling by the CMO Club Awards, and was named a "Top Ten Most Interesting B2B Executives" among other accolades. Since I started my own company, Tenshey, to advance diverse talents in the workplace, we were awarded for diversity innovations with our sponsorship programs specifically built for professional women.

But this story isn't about me - it's about you.

My ascension to the C-suite, and my industry recognitions are what people see from the outside. The same is true for other executives. What they don't see is our journey to get there, the triumphs and struggles, the tough decisions and the thought processes. In this book, I want to share these stories with you and hope that even if you get one idea, it will be worth it.

I was navigating a male-dominated world where women comprised only 20% of all C-level roles, and women of color was at a mere 4%. Throughout my time in corporate America, I encountered dozens, even hundreds, of talented, hardworking, ambitious women who felt like their contributions weren't recognized or that they had not found a way to advance their careers to their potential. Given that women account for nearly half of the labor force, that stat just didn't sit right with me. As I dug deeper, I found out that women were demonstrably promoted at a slower rate, despite having the same hunger and drive of their male counterparts.

My decision to step off my corporate track onto entrepreneurship was motivated by my desire to help ambitious, capable women and underrepresented minority talents to realize their career goals. I wanted to give ambitious women the coaching, guidance, and support to grow their careers. But I wasn't just helping these women – I was helping the companies that they worked for to become more inclusive.

In a 2018 study, BCG found that companies with above-average diversity in their management teams reported a 19% boost in revenue due to better innovation. McKinsey confirmed those findings in their 2020 study "Diversity Wins: How Inclusion Matters" where they concluded that companies in the top quartile for ethnic and gender diversity were 36% more profitable than companies in the bottom quartile.

This all led me to found Tenshey, and eventually to write this book. It's become my personal mission to advance gender diversity and leadership development in the workplace so that the next generation of the C-suite will look more equitable and foster inclusivity and belonging for all.

MY LIGHT BULB MOMENT

All in all, I had been in tech for over 20 years, and if you know anything about working in tech, you know that it's like dog years. The time I spent at SAP was one of the most rewarding career experiences of my life. I led a global team of 1,300 employees serving 180 countries and we were collectively responsible for marketing the multi-billion dollar behemoth.

My leadership team was a 50/50 split of women and men, and 40% were ethnic minorities. That was rare in the tech industry. During my tenure at SAP, from 2014 to 2017, revenue rose 33.5% to 23.5 billion euros. Over the same period of time, SAP's share price rose 71%. The role, as expected, was intense - chock full of conference calls, international flights, and being "on" around-the-clock. In the summer of 2017, after almost three years, I felt it was time to leave the company.

For the very first time in my career, I was taking a break, a real break. While calls were pouring in for other CMO opportunities, I was determined to spend quality time reconnecting with friends and family, and recharging my own "batteries". I learned how to wake surf, and spent a lot of time with my husband, and our miniature poodle Charlie, on our boat. I spent time walking in the park with my mom. I travelled to see friends, and even made a surprise visit to my Uncle Louis' 60th birthday family trip to Hawaii. I realized just how intense my career was and how I didn't take the time to stop and spend time with my family. There was always just one more email to respond to, one more conference call to attend, one more project to finish. I came to the ultimate realization that I was missing out on the relationships that I cared so much about.

The next big question I asked myself was "What's next?"

That fall, I was asked to speak to a group of executive MBA students at Cornell. Since that's where I got my MBA, I enthusiastically accepted the invitation. When I got there they asked me "Maggie, you've had such an amazing career, were mentors, coaches, and sponsors important in your career growth?" My response was "Absolutely! They were all instrumental in my growth. In fact, I started working with an executive coach eight years ago when I was a director at Microsoft."

That conversation got me thinking, "Why weren't more emerging leaders or even female executives getting the same support that I got when I was growing my career?"

Women and minorities are notoriously underrepresented in executive leadership positions, so why don't they have access to resources that can help them? As I thought about it more, a lightbulb moment ensued. I asked myself "How can I connect more women with executive coaches who can help them grow?"

That moment served as the deciding factor for me to turn my personal values into a business and was the launching point for Tenshey. My goal was to provide leadership development and executive coaching for women so that they could have access to the same resources that helped me advance my career.

But all of the coaching, mentoring, and sponsorship in the world won't help you unless you know what you want and where you're going.

THE KEY TO EXCITEMENT, EXPLORATION, AND OPPORTUNITY

Sailors have been navigating the open ocean via the stars for hundreds, even thousands, of years. The stars, chiefly the North Star, guided weary sailors through wayward waters and unfamiliar territory. The North Star, unlike any other star in the sky, remains stationary throughout the entire night, making it a reliable landmark in the sky by which travelers could chart their course.

What makes the North Star so unique is not only that it remains stationary in the night sky, it's that the Earth is pointed directly at it, meaning that if you look at the North Star at any time of night, it points North. If you were at the equator, the North Star would be at the horizon. If you were at the North Pole, the North Star would be directly overhead.

Why is this so important? Because it was a reliable indicator of direction, no matter where you are in the world. And in many ways, it's the perfect analogy for your career.

Before I got my CMO job at SAP, I had already decided that I wanted that role in a tech company – seven years before it ever happened. What I didn't know at the time was the size of the company and where that opportunity would come from. That's the transformative power of defining your North Star.

Defining your career North Star is about finding your passion. It's about knowing yourself and knowing what really excites you. It's about exploring your strengths, your weaknesses, and what you want to learn. It's about exploring what you want to do, what you want to accomplish, and ultimately who you want to become. It will look different depending where you are in your career, where you are in your life, and whether you're early on in your career or a seasoned veteran.

If you're just starting out in your career, there are so many things that you may not even know about yourself. You haven't worked many jobs and you haven't had the experience to know yourself yet. Knowing yourself is about getting to experience different types of roles in different types of projects. School internships are a great way to go about this. While you're in school, just starting out, or even when you're just getting out of school and graduating.

During this time, it's good to take stock of the things that make you get up in the morning. What excites you? What do you dread? For some people it's, "Oh my gosh, if I have to create another spreadsheet, I'll die." Or they're the opposite and they love crunching numbers in Excel and pivot tables excite them. It's about getting to know yourself and the things that excite you. In other words, the things you want to do more of.

You want to be intentional about looking for those types of opportunities as you grow your career. What type of roles give you excitement or give you challenges that excite you? Equally important, what are the roles that you would rather skip? If 80% of your time is doing something you don't enjoy, that's not the path you want to go down. I thought I was going to work in finance because I was really good at math, but it wasn't my passion. Once I was introduced to marketing, I fell in love with it.

I can't overstate the importance of exploring new things so that you can unearth your passions. My newfound passion for marketing led me to where I am today and I'm so thankful that I had the opportunity to discover it.

I remember Professor Berger talking about how companies build brands in my first undergraduate marketing course at Binghamton University in Upstate New York. He discussed understanding consumer behavior, recognizing consumer needs, and how to create a strategy around that. I quickly found that those were the things that excited me. So when I went into the workforce, marketing was precisely what I wanted to do so I could put what I learned in my marketing classes into practice.

One of the things I love doing when I mentor people, especially if they're early in their career or an intern, is to have career development conversations. Whenever I speak with college or MBA interns, they always ask "How do I choose the *right* job?"

If you're unclear about what you want to do fresh out of college, there are no wrong choices. In fact, if you haven't yet discovered your passion, that's ok too. I always say that when you're first out of school, there's no such thing as a "wrong" job. Your first is just a starting point - and you can't judge yourself, or even your job when you're just starting out. Like many before you, you'll most likely end up in a different type of function or profession altogether than where you started. So don't write off a job before you give yourself time to feel it out and awaken a dormant interest.

A DAY IN THE LIFE

Another question I often get when mentoring young talents is, "How do I choose a role, or what should I do if I'm interested in a "fill in the blank" role?" I always advise them to talk to the people who are currently in those roles so they get a sense of what it's like before they make the commitment to it. That way you can check back in with yourself and gauge if it excites you and if it aligns with your passions and interests.

When I was at Microsoft back in 2006, I remember being interested in a business development role. It was a role that focused on building strategic partnerships with other companies. I happened to know one of the business development managers so I reached out and asked him "Can I buy you a cup of coffee and pick your brain about your role? I'm thinking of applying but I wanted to get a better sense of the role itself first." I enjoyed working with partners from my early days at Sun Microsystems, so this role seemed right up my alley. I loved the idea of collaborating with other companies, so it seemed like an ideal role. When I met with him, one thing stood out for me. He explained that while collaborating with partners and mapping out strategy was a big part of the role, another part of it had to do with lengthy sessions in reviewing legal contracts, and negotiating terms.

That was a lightbulb moment for me because pouring over contracts was just not my superpower nor my cup of tea. He explained that quite a bit of his time was spent doing just that. Once I realized that I'd be spending a significant chunk of time doing work that I wouldn't enjoy as much, I was able to shift gears and pursue other opportunities. Eliminating options is a great way to help you find what you want.

That's why I recommend that my mentees learn as much about a position as possible, especially if it's an internal position. The insights you gain are invaluable and can seriously affect your satisfaction at work. It's a big loss for everyone if you end up getting a position that you ultimately don't like.

On the other hand, when I have people approach me about a career in marketing and I see that excitement in their eyes, I feel so much more comfortable advocating for them and helping them get one of those roles.

Another piece of advice I often share is for them to ask what it takes to succeed in that role. You can ask what qualifications you need, how they got into their roles, what books you can read, what conferences or online training you should attend to do that role really well. Everyone respects someone that's well prepared. Thinking about how you can position yourself as a strong candidate will work wonders. That level of seriousness and preparation will impress whoever it is that you're asking and will increase the likelihood that they'll help you get this role.

One of the perks of starting out at a larger organization is the job rotation programs that some of them offer. This is where college and MBA graduates actually rotate between multiple jobs in two years so that they experience different functions and jobs within an organization. The goal is to help them learn about different parts of the company and to eventually land a job that's the best fit for them and the group. Sadly, the majority of people, myself included, never really had an opportunity to experience a job rotation program. If that's you, just try different roles so you learn how the company operates and more importantly, to learn about yourself.

I spent the first 10 years of my career trying out different roles within marketing. Even within marketing, there are a myriad of different roles, each with their own distinct responsibilities; from product management, to product marketing, to channel marketing, to field marketing, to strategic marketing, to corporate marketing. Marketing is a broad discipline and there was no shortage of opportunity.

I tried different types of roles to learn new areas and find out which fit best. One thing that I noticed when transitioning from product management to product marketing to partner marketing, is that I really loved the engagement with customers and partners. From then on, every single role that I took had to give me the chance to spend time externally with customers and partners as well.

BE INTENTIONAL

Years ago, I was on the campus at Cornell University attending the annual PCCW event (President's Council of Cornell Women). It's a group of highly accomplished alumni working to enhance the involvement of women students, faculty, staff, and alumni as leaders within Cornell University. The summit was held in the spring, attended by a group of around 150 women including Council members like myself, and current students both graduates and under-graduates.

I remember we were in the ballroom for a lunch panel with the students and one of the questions we were asked was "How important is it to pick the "right" job out of college?"

I remember because it was during spring and the seniors were starting to decide which path they were going to take. They were deciding which company, which job, and every-thing that goes along with that. I could sense their anxiety. In response, the moderator asked the following question to all the Council members in the room, "How many of you changed careers since your first job out of school?" A major-ity, if not all, of the people, myself included, raised our hand.

That tells you that you should pick the job that you feel like you connect with the most – the job itself, the culture of the company, and most importantly the hiring manager. There's a saying that "People don't leave a company, they leave the manager". There's a lot of truth to it. You're very likely going to pivot to a different career somewhere down the line as you learn more about yourself anyway. You'll have different interests, which will lead you down different career paths - and that's ok. The students looked so relieved to know that the pressure they felt to make the "right" choice was not as severe as they had thought.

Eventually, as you get to know yourself better, or as your interests change, or your life situation changes, you'll consider a different path. You don't have to feel like every career decision is a "make or break" moment where you have to absolutely pick the "right" one. You can truly choose your starting point from anywhere.

That's why I advise people to always be intentional. It's just that you're intentional for different reasons. When you are freshly out of school and looking for jobs, you're intentional about wanting to learn different things you are interested in. You'll want to learn about different types of roles, different types of functions, different industries, and even different sizes of companies. Or if you're in a startup, you're most likely wearing multiple hats anyway which gives you broad experience. That all gives you a broader sense of how different parts of an organization function. It also gives you a chance to see what things you like, and which things that you don't.

I remember being ten years into my career and up to that point, I was either changing roles in a lateral move or getting promoted every 18 to 24 months. That's just me. I tended to want to get through my learning curve quickly so I could be a contributing member of the team. By the time I hit the 18-24 month mark, I would feel that I had accomplished what I had set out to do in that role and was ready for the next challenge. Of course, as you grow higher into an organization, that time span will stretch longer and longer as the roles become more complex, but being intentional in the roles you take and what you want to accomplish in the role is key.

It was 2006. I was a group manager at Microsoft. I was about 18 months in the company and ready to look for my next position. I applied for a number of different positions within Microsoft, from a field marketing manager role to a business operations role. I should mention that while I had a ton of ambition, I didn't have a coherent strategy to govern it. I was still in the mindset of learning new skills through different roles.

Apparently, my unfocused approach caught the attention of my VP, my manager's manager. So he approached me and said "Maggie, what do you want to do? What is your career North Star?" I had no idea how to respond, and my blank stare must have given away my response. He went on to say "What do you want to be when you grow up? Go home and think about it and come back and tell me." That was a pivotal moment. It was the first time that I really stopped to think not about just what I'm going to do in terms of today, or even in terms of my next role. It stopped and made me ask myself "What am I going to do long term?"

Being a "Softie", a slang term for Microsoft employees, I went home and put a PowerPoint slide together. The next day, I came back and I had built my first version of a career roadmap. In my line of work as a product marketer at Microsoft and previously at Sun Microsystems, we were used to building product roadmaps. We'd map out how we'd build new products, what features we would include, and when the product would ultimately be "feature complete". Then we'd restart the whole process again for the next generation of products and capabilities.

I had done it for tech products, but interestingly enough, I had never used that approach for my own career. So I took some time to map out what I really wanted to do. Armed with my freshly minted career roadmap, I knew that I wanted to continue to grow and climb the corporate ladder within the marketing function. I told myself that my career roadmap is "feature complete" when I eventually lead an entire marketing organization for a company.

Back then it wasn't called a CMO, but that was what I was describing that I wanted to do. By then, I had a few roles in marketing and I knew I LOVED marketing. I knew deep down that this was the career path I wanted to pursue.

Identifying that I wanted to be a CMO one day was an important moment for me and my career. This milestone really helped me start thinking intentionally about my next role in the company, and what that would exactly look like. I thought about the competencies I would need to develop and the experiences I'd need under my belt. Then I'd be able to confidently say "Yes, this is the experience that is going to prepare me to become a CMO one day."

From that point forward I felt like my career was very intentional in the steps that I took to help me to eventually become a CMO. Little did I know, that opportunity would come a lot faster and bigger than I had thought.

THE MYTH OF THE LINEAR CAREER PATH

There's a cartoon of a CEO and CFO talking. The CFO says "Why are we spending money to develop these people? What happens if we invest in developing our people and they leave us?" The CEO looks at him and says "What happens if we don't and they stay?"

A lot of managers worry about losing their employees after they spend time developing them. It's an understandable concern, but I've found that great managers don't think like that.

I started my career in purchasing at ADIC because I couldn't find a job in marketing. I didn't want to, but it makes a better story to tell now. Two and a half years later, I finally got a marketing position within the company.

In that time, which was my first job out of college, I had grown from a junior buyer, which is the lowest you can get within the purchasing department, to eventually becoming a buyer, and then ultimately being promoted to a senior buyer within that two-and-a-half-year span.

That experience validated that there is NO wrong choice in your first job. I couldn't get into marketing, but when I look back at it, I was exactly where I needed to be. ADIC was a small, fast growing tech company at that time. It got me into the tech industry and allowed me to hone my skills.

Despite being in the purchasing department, my manager, Peter Hews, was supportive of me going into marketing. He had worked under the CEO, Peter van Oppen who had a habit of rotating his executives to different functions within the organization. He wanted them to have exposure to all aspects of the business so they could make more informed decisions. Because my manager was trained in that mindset, he thought it was a good idea for me to get experience in other parts of the organization, even if it meant losing me.

With Peter's support, I eventually landed in a marketing position, a position which was the genesis of my career North Star.

I understand the fear of letting go of great talent, but I've found that "exporting" talent out of your group serves as a badge of honor rather than a battle scar. Building great talent is what a leader is supposed to do.

FAST GROWTH COMPANIES

Peter van Oppen, the CEO of ADIC used to say that fast growth companies present the best growth opportunities for younger talent. My career growth under his leadership is a testament to that.

Back in 1997, in the middle of the dot-com bubble, ADIC was growing tremendously. The Seattle of that time was an iconic era known for Kurt Cobain, Ken Griffey Jr, and grunge rock. The war for technical talent was starting, but was nowhere as fierce as it is today.

In a lot of ways, I was incredibly lucky to be there. I was able to get my foot in the door of a fast growing tech company, and rode that wave my entire career. I have no idea what my path would have looked like if I wasn't there at that time.

Peter van Oppen was right, you're more likely to grow your career faster in an early stage, fast growth company. You're presented with innumerable opportunities and have to learn to make decisions very quickly. You're often working directly with the leadership team and given the freedom to make decisions independently, honing your instincts and preparing you to lead your own team in the future. But it's not right for everyone.

Working for larger companies with a solid reputation may not give you broad exposure to the business, but it gives you more depth in a specific role, more exposure to process, structure, and likely more formal leadership development training. These are a few of the tradeoffs to working for a hyper growth company versus an established one.

From experience, if you want to grow fast, a smaller company is the way to go. But if you want to learn driving scale, bigger corporations will be a better fit. It's good to try them both and see what fits you the best.

It's natural to think that you have to constantly move up in a nice linear, predictable curve. But that's just not how it is. As you continue to grow your career, you'll find that the roles and responsibilities you have become more complex, so you have to stay in your current position for longer to develop the skills and experience you need to do your job well - let alone do another job at the next level. You're also focusing on a longer term horizon for the company so it will take you longer to get to the results that you're looking for.

At the same time, you're competing against a much more sophisticated talent pool - against people who may have more experience than you. At this level, it's not only proficiency and skill that matter, it's breadth, perspective, and exposure to other business units that will factor into the hiring decision. Instead of trying to grow in a straight line, you want to start building out a broad set of experiences as you go up the career ladder.

That's why I advise people that it's not just about going up in a linear model. It's really about going up AND across so that you have broader foundational knowledge and competencies as you climb up the ladder. This breadth of expertise will help you to get a broader perspective on the business. Having a career North Star puts it all into context.

FOLLOWING YOUR HEAD VS FOLLOWING YOUR HEART

Sometimes that means putting your growth plan on hold so you can retool. That's exactly what I did back in 2007 when I geared up for my MBA. It was late 2006 and I had been at Microsoft for about two years. At that time my VP asked me to stay in the Worldwide Small Business group because he thought I was good at my job. It was an honor to be recognized like that and I thought "Wow, my executive asked me to stay." And of course the logical part of me, told myself that I needed to stay because I was told this is what I should do.

I knew deep down in my heart I wanted to explore other parts of marketing within the company. But in my head, it made perfect sense, because my executive asked me to stay, so that's what I did. My head won. I quickly realized that I had made the wrong decision. It was wrong in a way that I don't regret because it taught me a lesson that would serve me well in the future. That lesson was "Given the chance to follow your head or follow your heart, always follow your heart." It was a valuable lesson that I needed to learn firsthand.

Now I know that I should always trust my gut, but at that moment, I decided to stay. As fate may have it, that role itself and even the product that I was supporting was just way ahead of its time. It was called Office Live, a suite of offerings that helped small businesses to build their online presence. But at that time, the internet was not as prominent as it is now for small businesses. To give you some context, that was the time before the first Apple iPhone was even launched. Small businesses didn't need to have a website back then especially considering how slow internet speeds were. It was a little bit ahead of its time to get the traction it needed in the market.

On top of that, I wasn't really happy in the role. So I remember that a few years prior, I was thinking about getting an MBA. I started looking at MBA programs and came across the Cornell Executive MBA program that had a hybrid learning model for working professionals. It was the second year that they were recruiting in Seattle for the Seattle cohort. It was a primarily long-distance program that lasted for 18 months. It allowed students to mostly take classes remotely while still maintaining a classroom-based model, and combined with an on-campus component.

We would spend two weeks on campus three times during the program, but the rest of the classes were done via video conference. We spent a whole day on Saturday in a video-conference classroom, which they call a boardroom. I was thrilled to have gotten into an Ivy League school. I'm the first person in my family who earned a college degree, and I would also be the first person in my family to get a graduate degree. I visited Cornell's campus in Ithaca New York once when I was a college student at Binghamton and I remember thinking, "That's where the super smart kids go." I had a similar thought when I first visited the Microsoft campus with a friend who worked there while I was working at ADIC. I thought, that's where the super smart people work. I never thought I was smart enough to attend an Ivy League school or to work at a company like Microsoft. But what I realized years later was that I might not qualify for something at one moment in time, but that doesn't mean that opportunity is gone forever. With hard work, tenacity, and a bit of luck, those opportunities may very well be within your reach.

When I was about to start my MBA, I was also debating a new role within Microsoft. One of them was a partner strategy role for the Server & Tools Business Unit, a role that I knew what to expect and I was confident I would do a good job in. Another role was also a partner strategy role but for this brand new category of "Services" product that would eventually be coined Cloud Services and SaaS.

My head convinced me that I should choose a tried and true role in the Servers & Tools Business Unit because I would essentially have two full time roles – a working professional and a student. But my heart told me that being on the ground level launching a new category of products is the exact big challenge that would excite me. I was working on this new set of products on a stretch project for the three months prior so I knew the heavy demand of this newly created role. I discussed my concern of my own bandwidth to take on this demanding role with the hiring manager, Gretchen. Not only was Gretchen very understanding, she also vowed to support me in my quest of my MBA study.

This time my heart won. I decided to start a new full-time job and a new executive MBA program at the same time.

It was a big commitment, but ultimately it was the right thing for me. Committing to a graduate program is already a big undertaking, and adding a full time job on top of it was a huge challenge. But it was a goal of mine, so I persevered through it. I remember talking to Barbara, one of my early mentors at Microsoft and she asked me "Maggie, are you doing this Executive MBA program for your job? For your career advancement? Or what is this for?" And I said, "I want to do this because this is a personal commitment. I was the first person in my family to graduate from college and I wanted to be the first person in my family to graduate from grad school as well. I also believe that going through this MBA program will give me more tools in my tool set. I'm always doing things the way that I've always done things, and going through the program may open up more new ideas, and new frameworks in my mind." She then said "Okay, that's good. Because if you were telling me that you're doing this MBA for your job, I would tell you not to. Because getting an MBA may not necessarily mean that you're going to get to a higher level. But doing it because you personally want to do it is the right thing to do."

I get asked a lot on whether and when one should consider an MBA, or postgraduate education of any kind. My answer is always, "It depends." It depends on what you're looking to achieve. Some may get an MBA to gain more formal business education for a career pivot. Others may see it as a personal goal like I did. Getting an MBA is a major investment so I suggest that you find out whether your employer offers any tuition reimbursement. It is also important to have an understanding with your family too because it would impact them as well.

In my case, I knew getting an MBA wouldn't necessarily translate to career advancement because I had already built my credibility within the organization. My advancements would be a result of my work performance. What I learned later was that when I ventured out to other organizations, an MBA was table stakes and a good checkmark on my resume.

To say my schedule was grueling was an understatement. I would go to work, get off around six, switch over to meet with my classmates to work on group projects. I'd get home around 8:30pm and then start reading for class. By about 11pm, I would switch back over to work to finish any business that I needed to do that day. On Saturdays I had class from 6:30am to 3:30pm because the professors were on the East coast doing video conferencing across "classrooms" or we called them "boardrooms" in the US and Canada. I was absolutely exhausted, so by the time Sunday rolled around, all I could really do was just sleep.

During those 18 months, especially in the beginning, I was fried. I always work hard, but I wasn't used to this kind of schedule. One thing I can say is that it forced me to learn how to brutally prioritize my time. I prioritized sleep, my job at Microsoft, and then my classwork (not in that order!)

That was the very first time in my career that I put my career on the backburner so I could retool myself. The problem is I didn't know how to do that. It was tough because in a sense I felt like I was just failing at my job. I wasn't really failing, but I was definitely not at my peak performance. I also felt like I was failing in school because I was having a hard time with the Business Decisions class which involved statistics and probabilities. The professor loved asking the class if we heard the pin drop in a way to see if we understood what he was teaching. I was thinking,

"I didn't even know where the pin was dropped!" That class was so intimidating that I even felt like I was going to flunk out of the program, so I was enormously stressed.

I couldn't go on as is - I knew that in order for me to both have a full-time job and be enrolled in an intensive MBA program simultaneously, something had to give. So I had to make adjustments.

I told myself that it's okay that I don't get an A in all of my classes and it's okay if I don't get stellar reviews at work. I reluctantly came to terms with the idea that getting a "B" or even a "B minus" in both school and my career would be ok - at least for the next 18 months. For an "overachiever" like me, it was hard to come to terms with that. I had to remind myself that not everything can be a priority at the same time.

This reminds me that, in the height of the COVID-19 pandemic, I was giving a virtual speech at a women's leadership event of a Fortune 100 company. I shared this exact story with the audience. A mom in the audience shared this in the chat window "such a great message - as a mom with 5 young children, I have to remind my (competitive) self that it is OK to not always be moving forward/upward - as much as I may want to. Giving yourself the permission that it is okay is huge! Just be sure to check in with yourself often when it is time to re-engage and re-calibrate your priorities." That was spot on! Just like what many of us do at work, sometimes you have to adjust your priorities as the business environment changes. Why wouldn't we do the same to manage our careers and personal lives as well?

TAKE THE ROAD LESS TRAVELLED

At the end of the day, I took the road less travelled and it made all the difference in the world. Earlier I spoke about the difficult lesson I had to learn between following my head and following my heart - from that point on I always listened to my heart and followed my passions.

I would say, sometimes what I see happening at work is everyone wants to get on the hottest project, with the most cutting-edge product, on the most high-profile team. Don't get me wrong, those projects are fun.

That said, it can also be very rewarding to take on projects that are less visible or technologies in such nascent stages that they fly below the radar for most people. I've found that when you take on something new, the payoff is usually much bigger. But frankly, it's mostly because of my curiosity and desire to learn new things.

I mentioned the Office Live team I was on when I was contemplating the Executive MBA program. The product wasn't quite ready for primetime. But because I was on that team, it got me onto the Cloud Services area, which took place during the very, very early days of cloud computing at Microsoft.

It was impactful for me because I was always drawn to work on emerging projects. They're more risky because not all emerging technologies or projects take off, but when they do , the payoff is huge.

It was right at the culmination of the cloud computing revolution, and was a pivotal moment for Microsoft as they were transitioning from a traditional on-premise software company to a cloud provider. Like a surfer paddling out to sea, positioning herself for a big wave, I couldn't tell you when that big wave would come, but when it did, I wanted to be ready to ride it. I knew that this move would have a massive impact on the entire industry when it was forced to reinvent itself and take cloud computing seriously. I wanted to have a front row seat to this massive evolution. Luckily for me, it also had an immeasurable impact on my career trajectory.

That's why I'm so passionate about emerging trends and love the risk and reward associated with them. I like taking big risks, because even though there's no guarantee of success, the act of taking that risk on a path that no one has been on before can lead to life-changing benefits down the line.

Whether you work at a startup, or work on an emerging product within your company - taking that leap can position you really, really well. Just look at Jeff Bezos who left a comfortable Wall Street job, borrowed money from his parents, and started an online bookstore called Amazon.com He was living a great life but pioneered an entirely new company, disrupting businesses forever. It's hard to overstate the impact that Jeff Bezos made by deciding to take the road less travelled and blazing his own trail. That said, for every trillion-dollar Amazon.com, there are a trail of failed companies that didn't fare so well. So taking a massive bet and choosing the road less travelled is no guarantee of success.

No matter what you decide to do, I always advise people to listen to your heart, trust your gut, and chase your passions. That's the only way you'll make it through the long haul. Sure, "Follow your passion" sounds cheesy but the truth is that following your passion isn't for the good days, it's for the bad ones. The days you feel like every move you made led you to nowhere. The days when you feel everything is falling apart. The days when you feel that you're not progressing the way you were expecting.

Following your passions gives you a reason to push past the pain, the fear, the disappointment, and the frustration to continue on this path. Even if it doesn't work out, you still feel you gave it your all and are able to extract lessons along the way. If you never were passionate, you'll hate every minute of it and may never discover those valuable lessons along the way - if that's the case, then it's a fruitless endeavor.

UNDER PROMISE, OVER DELIVER

One of the pieces of advice I give people, especially early talent, is to under promise and over deliver. We all get really excited about certain projects and want to make an impression on our superiors. Carried away by our own enthusiasm, we tend to overestimate our capabilities and underestimate the complexity of the work. In the process, we commit to unrealistic deadlines that we fail to adhere to. In reality, if we were to scope out the task at hand, we'd realize that it would take a lot more effort or that there were other "curveballs" than we originally thought.

But since we've committed to a certain timeframe, we now have two choices; we can do whatever it takes to hit the deadline so that we don't hurt our credibility, or we end up delivering the project late or with substandard quality, ultimately tarnishing our reputation. Neither scenario is ideal.

The advice I share with people is to under promise and over deliver. If you don't feel like you have enough information about a project, or if you feel that the scope is too big, it's ok to say "I'd like to scope out the project a bit more and get back to you with a date that I can commit to."

For example, if in your estimate that you can get the project done in three days, ask yourself, have you given yourself a buffer of any unforeseen issues. There may be pieces of data you need from someone else or certain research you must do is still undefined. By no means am I suggesting you to "sandbag" and set a lower expectation because they will negatively impact your credibility. If all the elements are under your control, you should commit to completing the project at your estimated schedule.

My point is that for most projects, there are certain elements that are out of your control and therefore, you need to add them to your estimate. Managing expectations and setting realistic timelines will help you achieve your goals and build your credibility.

The hallmark of a great employee is someone who is reliable and can commit to getting a project done properly and on time. Establishing that habit early in your career will differentiate you from others within the organization.

So commit to the deadline, and if you need more time to research the time needed for the project, ask if you can get back to them with a date. You can use softening language like "I'd love to get this done as soon as possible, but I don't want to overcommit. May I get back to you with a date tomorrow?" That simple statement can save you a lot of grief and position you as someone with integrity.

There also will be times when something unforeseen happens that impacts your ability to deliver on time. Whether you have a personal matter in your life or whether someone else that you're relying on fails to do their part, mishaps happen. The key in those situations is to notify your superiors as early as you can so that they can temper their expectations of you and also expectations they might have set with others. In these scenarios, I find that you need to over communicate because no one likes surprises. The earlier you notify them the better. As long as you explain what happened and more importantly, what you're doing to fix it, you'll build trust and credibility. People will respect you for having hard conversations up front rather than surprising them at the last minute.

THREE FOCUSES, ONE LEAD AT A TIME

When I think about my own career, I think about three important elements that intertwine with each other like a Venn diagram. The three things that always come back up in my decisions are:

What are my professional aspirations?

What is my financial goal?

What is my personal purpose?

In the early days of my career, my focus was always on my professional growth. I was ambitious and thought about what I needed to do to grow my career. Leaders trusted me to take on big challenges because I was reliable. When I committed to a project, I would work days and nights to ensure that I could deliver high quality work and hit the deadlines. I remember being at Sun Microsystems back in 2000 when I was in my mid-twenties, and I was talking with one of my colleagues on the marketing team. She was a mom of two young children and we were just having a casual chat when she said "You know, Maggie, I can see that you're very ambitious, I can tell you, once you have a family, your priorities will change."

And I said, "I don't think that's going to be me. I could only see that my focus will always be my career."

That conversation stayed in my mind because my priorities did change over the years. But no one could tell my twenty-something self that. In fact, I found that some advice I received over the years didn't resonate until I personally experienced that particular situation. Nevertheless, I "filed" it in my memory bank.

In 2012, I had completed my time at Microsoft and decided to go to Level 3. That was my entry point as a senior executive at a Fortune 500 company. I was in my late thirties and started talking with one of my colleagues, who was also a senior executive who was in his fifties at the time. I remember telling him, "You know what, I want to retire by the time I turn fifty." He retorted "What? What are you talking about? I mean, I'm in my fifties, and retirement is not even in my vocabulary." I replied, "Well, I want to have the freedom to do what I want to do."

I shared that conversation with my manager Andrew at the time and he said "Maggie, I don't think you're saying you want to retire by the time you turn fifty. I think you're saying that you want to be financially independent, so you have the freedom to choose what you want to do." And that really got it in my head. I said, "Yes, that's exactly what I want!"

At that point, I was well on my way to achieve my professional goals, being in a senior executive position at a Fortune 500 company, and steadily making progress toward my ultimate goal of stepping into the role of Chief Marketing Officer. That's when I decided to prioritize my financial goals so that I could achieve the financial independence that I so very much wanted.

The good news was that back in 2012, I found Jennifer, my financial advisor, to help my husband and me plan our finances. Shortly after my conversation with Andrew, my husband and I talked to our financial advisor Jennifer and mapped out a plan to achieve financial independence.

I realized the importance of having a professional help me with our finances in a lesson I had to learn the hard way years prior. I dabbled in stock investing through online trading when I first started my career. Because my "strategy" was to buy what was "hot" at the moment, I never spent the time to properly research the company's financial health and business model. Needless to say, I didn't do very well in my stock picks. I always joke with people that my investment strategy was to "buy high and sell low", which obviously was a losing proposition.

My husband and I have felt a connection with Jennifer right away. Both Jennifer and I emigrated from Hong Kong, and we liked her pragmatic, no "B.S." approach. Having a financial advisor put us on a path to reach our goal of achieving financial independence.

Like my colleague at Level 3, I didn't think "retirement" would be in my vocabulary. I have too much energy and a passion to learn new things. But reaching financial independence meant I could be free to pursue my passions. While I enjoyed most of my days as a marketer and a corporate executive, there were days I felt like the corporate bureaucracy and office politics were too much to bear. I wanted to have the freedom to know that I didn't need a job if I didn't want to. I wanted to be able to stay in a job because I loved what I did, not because I felt like I was stuck.

By the time I left SAP in 2017, I had achieved my professional goals, and reached financial independence. I was able to take a step back and spend time thinking about what I really wanted in life. My coach Mary and I had numerous, deep conversations about what I want to focus my time on. I kept searching my "memory bank" on things I did that made me happy. It always came back to people and leadership development.

When I see people, especially underrepresented minorities, seizing an opportunity to unleash their potential, that makes me happy. I thought "How can I help more women and people of color to grow within organizations? I've grown my career without seeing a lot of people that looked like me. I want the next generation to see something different. I want the next generation to see more equity and inclusion." That was it. That was my purpose. That's also why I let go of the corporate career that I spent so many years building to start my own company, Tenshey.

As I mentioned previously, these three goals are intertwined. I've always considered these three elements in my professional decisions. Anytime a choice needs to be made between the three, one will be the lead goal at any given time. That's why it's important to define your three focus areas: professional, financial, and purpose.

For example, I once met a very talented product marketing manager at Microsoft. We reconnected years later when he shared that he and his family decided to store all of his belongings and start traveling the world. He continued to work in marketing, but as a freelancer so he could work anywhere in the world. His "lead focus" was to experience the world and cultures together with his family.

Everyone's journey is different, everyone's aspirations are different, and everyone's values are different, but it's so, so important to define them for yourself and prioritize them so that you can be intentional in the decisions you make and the actions you take. That's what having a career North Star is all about.

It's ok for your focus areas to change and develop over time. In fact, it's inevitable that they will evolve over time. In my twenties it was all about career growth; I've always been an overachiever and I've always been competitive and driven. When I set my sights on something, I don't rest until I get it done.

In the early days, I wanted to grow my career, so that's what I focused on. Noticeably absent was a deeper sense of purpose. Interestingly, in my executive coaching work with Tenshey, I'm seeing a major shift in the market where people are identifying and pursuing their purpose much earlier than I ever did. It's so fun to talk to our employees and interns, who are millennials and Gen Zers that have such a mature and developed sense of purpose. Their mentality and mindset is years ahead of their age. It's inspiring because that sense of purpose will help them make quantum leaps, not only in their careers, but in their lives. They have a strong idea of what they want and the legacy they want to leave. They also have an idea on how they want to leave the world for the next generation. That long-term, generational, purpose-driven thinking is absolutely amazing and delightful to see.

Having a clear vision of your purpose, your values, and your career North Star will serve you well. That said, I'm all about focus. Work-life balance is a popular concept, but I'm not about work-life balance as much as I'm about work-life integration. The fact of the matter is that if you have a North Star and big, audacious goals, you'll have to pursue them with relentless passion; often at the expense of your social life (or as was my case during my MBA, sleep).

The question is, how do you plan every single piece of your life so that it works for you? There will be times that you're absolutely focused on your career and there will be times where you really want to spend time with your loved ones. There will be times where you'll have to decide between excelling at work and excelling in your education. There will be times where you'll have to decide between sharpening your craft or learning a new skill. There are no right answers to any of these choices, but just like a sailor from days of old forging through choppy waters on a dark night, they should all be guided by your goals, your vision, and your North Star.

If your goals and purpose are important enough to you, not only will you not mind sacrificing those aspects of your life, you'll enjoy the journey to get there. The pleasure, the pain, the heartbreak - it's just like adopting a puppy and loving feeding it, cleaning up its accidents, holding it at night when it's sad and whimpering. The pain becomes pleasure because you're doing something that's important to you.

Key Takeaways

- **Define Your North Star**: I was always passionate about marketing since college. I knew I wanted to be the CMO of a tech company one day and every move I made since then was guided by that. Your career North Star is a blend between your passion and your ambition. It's about knowing what really excites you. It can change over time, but it will guide your decisions so that you act out of purpose and passion rather than drifting from job to job without clear focus.
- **Be Courageous and Explore**: When I first entered college, I thought I'd end up working in finance, but when I was exposed to marketing, I fell in love with

it. If you're early in your career, have the courage to expose yourself to different disciplines and discover what you like, and what you don't. It can be scary, but there's real growth in courageously exploring the unknown.

- **There's No Such Thing as a Linear Career Path**: My first job was as a junior buyer - far from what I wanted. But it was an awesome experience that molded me into the professional I am today. Your first job does NOT define you. There will be bumps and detours and that's OK! Things won't always pan out the way you want, so enjoy the journey and connect with your passions.
- **Define Your "Lead" Focus**: I suggest that people define their professional goals, their financial goals, and their personal values. Early in my journey, my primary focus was my career. Once I was on my way to achieving my professional goal, I started thinking deeply about financial independence. And because I removed financial security as a barrier, I get to focus on my personal values of advancing diversity and equality. Your goals will impact the decisions you make, so define your "lead" focus so that you can make decisions that align with that.

2

WHAT IS SPONSORSHIP?

I t's a familiar scene that's played itself out since the dawn of time; an older, more experienced "master" takes a young protégé under his wing, grooming him for greatness.

This relationship is memorialized through some of the greatest movies of the past generation from The Karate Kid, to Star Wars, to The Matrix. The wise master shares his coveted secrets with just the right protégé - a protégé that is often unsure of himself and unaware of his dormant greatness. The protégé eventually embraces his greatness and even outshines the master.

As captivating and these stories are, I see them played out time and again in corporate America. I see bright, talented, ambitious young men and women, identified as high potential employees, swept up in management training programs. They are guided by senior executives with political capital to open doors to new opportunities.

It's a familiar pattern and I've seen how impactful it was to not only my career, but to countless other people that I've had the pleasure to work with over the years. I've come to know it for what it is - "sponsorship".

It's incredibly powerful, but sadly, it's not an even playing field. While women represent half of the workforce at the entry-level, in corporate America, only one in five C-level executives are women and only one in twenty-five are women of color. More on that later.

DEFINING SPONSORSHIP

Whether I'm speaking to a client or a group of students at a university, I'm often asked, "What is sponsorship and how is it different from mentorship or coaching?" I always respond by saying that "Sponsorship is a measurable partnership between a higher-level leader in an organization who exerts their political capital to help a high-potential protégé advance their career."

"Measurable? How?" you may ask.

A sponsor is a bridge between where you are now and growth opportunities that you wouldn't typically have access to. A sponsor actively backs a protégé through their career.

In other words, a sponsor leverages their relationships and reputation to pull you forward in your career. To put it even more simply, unlike a mentor or coach, a sponsor has "skin in the game" and risks their reputation to advance your career.

It's powerful.

But there's a problem. Through my time in corporate America, and now with my own company, I've found that women are often over-mentored and under-sponsored.

We've thought about that quite a bit at my company. I always tell people that a coach is a secret weapon. Coaches help you gain clarity on what you want to achieve and the steps you need to take to get it. My own executive coach, Mary, has been instrumental in my success. She's helped me see beyond my limiting beliefs and challenged me to push myself ever since I met her back in my Microsoft days. She's been indispensable to my career and it's hard to describe how much she means to me.

Mentors on the other hand, are typically leaders who have achieved what you're looking to achieve, or excel in a competency you're looking to acquire, but they don't necessarily exert their influence to advance you in your career. Think of a mentor as someone who is willing to show you the ropes, but who may not be in a position to endorse you for advancement opportunities.

Sponsors, mentors, and coaches do overlap, but they each serve a specific purpose in your career growth, as illustrated in the diagram below. Ideally you would have multiple sponsors and mentors at any given time in your career journey.

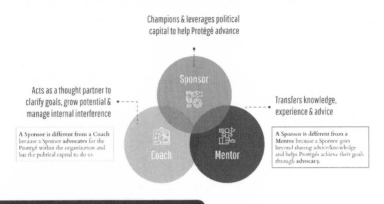

Champions & leverages political capital to help Protégé advance

Sponsor

Acts as a thought partner to clarify goals, grow potential & manage internal interference

A Sponsor is different from a Coach because a Sponsor advocates for the Protégé within the organization and has the political capital to do so.

Transfers knowledge, experience & advice

A Sponsor is different from a Mentor because a Sponsor goes beyond sharing advice/knowledge and helps Protégés achieve their goals through advocacy.

Coach

Mentor

Coach vs. Sponsor vs. Mentor

People tend to use the terms mentors and sponsors interchangeably, but there are some big differences. If mentors shine a light on the door for you, sponsors kick it open for you.

That's why I believe that sponsorship is the key to moving the needle for career advancement and leadership opportunities for anyone, but especially for women and people of color. Coaching and mentorship are crucial, but they lack the data-driven proof to propel women into leadership positions.

Sponsorship isn't new. In fact, sponsorship is what has gotten most men into leadership positions; the only difference is that it's often benefiting a subset of talents. And it only makes sense when you think of the heightened familiarity and relatability with other men in leadership positions at the company. If you look at CEOs in corporate America today, a majority of them would tell you that they ascended to the CEO role because a mentor took them under their wing and advanced them in their career. They may call that person a mentor, but when you look at the characteristics, it's usually a senior executive with political capital and connections that identified that up-and-coming person and groomed them for the current position. In other words, they are a sponsor.

The challenge is that a majority of the sponsorship relationships occurred between males. Sometimes it happens informally on the golf course. Sometimes it happens at airports and hotel lounges during business trips. Sometimes it happens at alumni associations where protégés and sponsors find common ground with each other. Over that time they discover shared interests, a similar background, and a greater level of trust with each other.

This isn't bad in and of itself. The problem is that women and underrepresented minorities often don't have the opportunity to have those interactions. It's not that they're less competent or less experienced; *it's that they're less visible.*

The few women and minorities that do receive (in)formal sponsorship are more the exception than the norm because most don't share the affinities that lead to the same level of visibility.

Most companies we work with, many of whom are large enterprises, were initially either unfamiliar with the term sponsorship or don't fully understand the impact that it can have on their company's values, culture, and innovation. The good news is that corporations have come to openly embrace diversity and inclusion as a business imperative and are realizing their tendency to gravitate to people that are similar to us, thanks to organizational data analytics. It's not difficult to see that many companies, especially in tech, financial services, oil & gas, and many others, are still struggling to gain traction in advancing underrepresented minorities in their leadership pipeline. As a result, organizations that are intentional about finding ways to break this cycle use sponsorship to identify protégés from diverse backgrounds. When they have the visibility and support from senior leaders previously, many seize the moment and get promoted as a result of their capabilities.

SPONSORSHIP AND "THE FROZEN MIDDLE"

Women, especially women of color, have long faced a disparity in executive level opportunities. As mentioned previously, according to McKinsey & LeanIn.Org's Women in the Workplace 2019 study, only "1 in 25 C-Suite executives is a woman of color." Corporations understand the need for greater Diversity, Equity, and Inclusion (DEI) in the workplace and yet, the needle has barely moved for women of color in senior executive positions.

On top of that, I've noticed that women struggle to advance past the "frozen middle" of mid-management positions because of the limited exposure they have to advancement opportunities compared to their male counterparts.

This inequity begins early on in women's careers and impacts them for a lifetime. According to McKinsey's and LeanIn.Org's *Women in the Workplace 2019* report, for every 100 men that were promoted or hired to manager, only 72 women were promoted or hired to the same position.

This "broken rung," caused by less women being promoted from entry-level positions, leads to fewer women in the leadership pipeline later on in their careers. As such, the number of women who would qualify for senior management positions is significantly lower than the men who qualify.

The more I thought about these statistics, the more I realized something bigger was at play. It's about visibility, network and advocacy - or lack thereof. That's why I believe sponsorship is such a critical tool to combat these problems.

Leaders in higher positions can change the game by sponsoring women so they have the visibility and advocacy to demonstrate their capabilities, earning a more equal chance to advance into higher positions.

If women and men were promoted to first-level managers at the same rates, one million more women would be added to management in corporate America over the next five years. If the gender gap was closed, we would add $28 trillion to the global economy by 2025 – the size of the United States and China's GDPs combined (*Bank of America Merrill Lynch 2019 report*).

Women of color in particular, need sponsors to cultivate strategic relationships. According to recent Korn Ferry research, "Nearly 60% of the Black executives who oversee major lines of business at Fortune 500 companies felt they had to work twice as hard - and accomplish twice as much - to be seen on the same level as their colleagues." Black women face even more unique challenges in that "49% feel that their race or ethnicity will make it harder for them to get a raise, promotion, or chance to get ahead, compared to just 3% of white women and 11% of women overall."

That said, diversity is just the first step in the long road toward equality. Since change often starts at the top, it's important for top leadership to set the example of inclusive leadership. Many well-respected organizations have shared their perspective on the traits of inclusive leaders. To me, the competencies of inclusive leadership include traits such as curiosity about others, emotional intelligence, and ability to adapt to new experiences.

Companies are increasingly hiring for diversity, yet the focus on inclusiveness and belonging, critical elements for retaining diverse talents, is still very much a work in progress. Inclusion is like the air we breathe, you cannot feel or touch it, but you know it's there. It's the difference between tokenism and true equality. It is not just simply being in the meeting; it's having your input valued and respected.

The common belief that if you train people with the right management skills, they will be equipped to grow successfully in their careers doesn't ring true. The reality is that the management conversations that take place behind closed doors matter. To that end, visibility matters. Interactions with people that have the political capital to move your career forward matter. Sponsors drive those conversations and advance career growth by leveraging their political capital to open the doors of opportunity.

WHY SPONSORSHIP WORKS

One thing is clear from our work with companies across the U.S. - diversity is a catalyst for growth and innovation - and sponsorship, done intentionally, can drive diversity, inclusion, and belonging.

In a 2018 report, Boston Consulting Group concluded that companies with above-average diversity on their management teams realized a 19% boost in revenue due to innovation. In another study, the Workforce Diversity Network cited that companies that prioritized diversity and inclusion initiatives had customer satisfaction scores 39% higher than those that didn't. Clearly, diversity and inclusion initiatives impact a company's financial performance.

Sponsorship creates a win-win for everyone involved. Sponsorship programs focusing on underrepresented minorities enhance organizational commitment to DEI (Diversity, Equity, and Inclusion), improves morale, speeds the pace of innovation, and leads to measurable financial gains.

Given the trend of protégés paying it forward and later becoming sponsors themselves, companies that make sponsorship a priority start to see a progression of diverse leadership in their pipeline as well. It's a virtuous cycle; a diverse leadership pipeline leads to more engaged employees who stay at the company longer and attract other talented resources.

Individual sponsors win because they align the company's actions with its commitment to diversity and inclusion. Along the way, they increase their own political capital by championing emerging leaders. Most importantly, they experience a boost in personal and professional satisfaction when they see their protégé advance to the next stage of their career.

I can tell you firsthand that seeing someone advance in their career, knowing I had a role in it, is an indescribable feeling.

Of course, protégés win because they gain access to opportunities that they might never have had before. They feel empowered and motivated because they've broken through the glass ceiling and are able to showcase their talent.

SPONSORS ADVOCATE FOR YOU

When I look back in my corporate career, any role that propelled me to a big step forward was always backed by one or more sponsors. They were my champions during the hiring process, whether it was creating a new role for me or advocating for me throughout the hiring process.

A great example is getting my dream job as CMO of SAP. I often get asked, "Maggie, how did you get the Chief Marketing Officer role at SAP?" For an executive role where an external executive recruiting firm is engaged, you typically must pass through that part of the process before speaking with the hiring company so that they present the most suitable candidates to the client.

This was the case for SAP. The C-level executive leading the CMO search was Stefan Ries, then Chief Human Resources Officer (CHRO) of SAP. Stefan is a forward thinker, an innovator in culture and organizational transformation, and has such a warm personality. When I first spoke with Stefan, we found common interests in technology transformation, as well as leadership development and diversity and inclusion. Towards the end of the interview, Stefan asked that I meet with Bill McDermott, then CEO of SAP as the next step. I was ecstatic.

When I prepare for an executive or a board interview, where most are public companies, I always read the company's annual reports, listen to their quarterly earnings calls, and find the latest news and articles both about the company and the executive(s) I would be meeting with. I always advise executives I mentor to go beyond the job description or specifications and dive in to understand what the company purpose is, their biggest opportunities for growth, and the "headwind" (challenges) they face. Then articulate the values you can bring to the table if you were hired. I would also check out company reviews on Glassdoor to see current and former employees' perspectives. Since culture is important to me, I take time to understand the company mission, vision, and values.

When I met Bill at SAP's North America Headquarters in Newtown Square, Pennsylvania, I was prepared. I did my homework and I knew how I could add value to the role – my value proposition. But I also know that this is a long shot for me. Such a coveted role would no doubt attract great talent including many who already have global CMO experience.

Since Bill was already a world-renowned CEO, I was able to find information about his vision for the company, his own leadership journey and principles on the internet. Bill is exactly what you see on his TV interviews. He's personable, inspirational, and known for his bold vision.

The interview was scheduled for an hour, but we ended up talking for almost two hours. In interviews, I always want to establish a personal connection. Knowing Bill bought and ran a deli when he was only a teenager, I shared my story of my solo flight to NY to start a new chapter of my life at the age of fourteen. We spent a lot of time discussing the cloud transformation that both the tech industry and SAP were embarking on and the lessons I had learned in the early cloud journey at Microsoft. About 45 minutes into the interview, Bill said to me, "Maggie, you have to join SAP." I was thinking, "Am I dreaming? Is this really happening?" One of the final questions I asked Bill during that interview was his advice for me if I were to be in the role, which I continue to follow. He said:

"Be the leader others want to follow
Be where the action is
Lead by example."

I then went on to interview with each of the Executive Board members and other critical stakeholders of the role. Both Bill and Stefan were incredible advocates for me throughout the process. For the three years I was at SAP, Bill was a key sponsor of mine and gave me an opportunity of a lifetime to be the steward of one of the world's most valuable brands. During my tenure, we had built the biggest and most comprehensive "Run Simple" campaign helping enterprises to combat complexity in their digital transformation journey and winning industry leading Effie awards for our marketing effectiveness in contributing to the brand's success. I will always be grateful to have been part of that.

Stefan was a key ally and sounding board. Our teams had so much fun partnering to evangelize the Employer brand, and supporting Stefan's "inner rocker" in his innovative creation of the HR Punks movement in transforming the HR function.

SPONSORS ACCELERATE YOUR CAREER GROWTH

Here's one of my favorite stories illustrating the power of sponsorship.

When I was the Chief Marketing Officer at SAP, the company already had a strong focus on gender diversity including a publicly stated target for women in leadership. I decided to initiate a pilot program in the global marketing organization to increase the number of women in the executive leadership pipeline.

During that process, I learned about a woman named Gail Moody-Byrd, a Senior Director on my marketing team. She was talented, hard-working, and doing a great job on our digital marketing initiatives - but she wasn't very visible within the organization. When her name bubbled up to me through her skip level manager Sian Smith, I reviewed her track record and decided to sponsor her.

I was intentional about sponsoring someone in an under-represented minority group. Women, let alone Black women, are severely underrepresented in tech. I wanted to do what I could to change that.

Up to that point, Gail had participated in various women leadership and mentorship programs in the company. She and her colleagues would meet once a month to discuss career goals and meet with skip level managers. She was ambitious and was rising through the ranks, but to Gail, it wasn't at the same pace when she compared herself to some of her peers.

When I decided to launch a pilot sponsorship program at SAP, I asked all my direct reports to come up with a list of people that they believed should be in this program. In order to participate in this sponsorship pilot, all protégés must be nominated by their leaders and Human Resource Business Partners as someone who is "ready now" or "ready in 12 months" for their next promotion as part of the annual talent calibration cycle - meaning they had demon-strated proven success in their role, and that they were ready to take on broader responsibilities for the company. Gail's name bubbled up through Sian.

She noticed an immediate difference when she joined the sponsorship program. Gail said to me, "Mentorship, as you know, is very different from sponsorship. The conversations with Sian, who was my skip-level manager at the time, completely changed from 'What are your ambitions?' to 'We need to establish a timetable for your promotion.'"

She went from casually discussing career goals with mentors and coaches, to gaining visibility and advocacy from myself and her skip-level manager via the deliberate sponsorship program I implemented.

Up to that point, Gail was very open about her ambitions. She was very clear with her manager, including her skip level manager, that she wanted a promotion. A few years later, when I interviewed her for this book and wanted to include her story, she told me "It's an interesting tightrope to walk though. Because you can be called out as being too ambitious, or too focused on your career."

She went on to say how she felt like she was called out for being ambitious rather than focusing on the job she currently had. "There are those kinds of questions that come up for women that I don't think typically come up from men, who can more freely talk about their ambitions. But I was pretty diligent about it over the years and made it known."

No matter what she did, she wasn't making the progress that she wanted in her career. She told me "I used to search through internal job boards, but it was incumbent on me as an individual to find and apply for those opportunities. But being in the sponsorship program, those opportunities were identified for me. I saw how roles in an organization are envisioned before they're even posted. I became privy to these opportunities before they were made transparent to the rest of the company." She went on to say "as I would have conversations with Sian about opportunities, I could tell there was a timetable. And she would talk about the need to get me in the right meetings."

She summed up her sponsorship experience by saying "I kind of became a partner with Sian in conversations about what the next step was for me and where the growth in the organization was. It was very specific. The meetings went from advice and counsel to an action plan with objectives."

It wasn't that she hadn't tried to grow on her own either. She opened up about the very real struggles she faced as a

Black woman in tech and told me, "I had been very careful to calibrate my behavior within the organization because I was once told that I was too ambitious."

She once told her manager that she dreamed of being CMO one day and was told that she needed to "dial that down". She went on to talk about the stereotype of the ambitious Black woman and how hard it was for her to walk the fine line of advocating for herself while simultaneously not drawing too much negative attention. At the same time, she knew that her very being as a Black woman innately drew attention to herself, so she felt there were limits to what she could do.

On the flip side, she didn't want to be viewed as the "affirmative action" candidate that got a position because of how she looked rather than the value she added to the organization. Knowing Gail, no one could ever make that accusation against her. She was an overachiever with a measurable track record of success – but still, the accusation of being an "affirmative action" candidate weighed on her psyche. As an Asian woman, I can identify with that feeling. I felt I always had to overachieve to prove that I earned my seat at the table.

In time, she was promoted to the Vice President level owning responsibility over web marketing including SAP's global website and 50 localized websites to deliver a digital-first customer experience as part of our customer journey. It was a major sense of accomplishment for her that led to immense career growth.

Over time, she reached her career North Star by taking on a CMO role at a fast growing startup focusing on enterprise artificial intelligence. But it didn't end there. Since then, she's been appointed to her first board of directors seat for a publicly-traded company – and I was one of her references.

The relationship that we built during our sponsorship program has stood the test of time.

Gail couldn't make me more proud. I always say that sponsors can open doors for you, but it's up to you to walk through them. Her success is a direct result of her work ethic and is a testament to the power of sponsorship.

I knew that diversity and inclusion were important to SAP and to me personally, so I made sure that I lived up to those ideals by creating this sponsorship program within the global marketing organization to sponsor an up and coming leader with a track record of success.

Lucky for me, a majority of the executives in the organization, like Sian, were inclusive leaders who embraced sponsorship and cultivated a diverse leadership pipeline. Out of the 30 women in the pilot sponsorship program, 50% of them had reported a positive progression in their career within a twelve-month period.

WHAT SPONSORS LOOK FOR

As a protégé, it's your job to be intentional about identifying potential sponsors and cultivating those relationships. You need to strengthen your competencies so that you're poised to take advantage of advancement opportunities when they're presented to you. And, you need to vocalize where you want to take your career. By doing so, others are more likely to be able to find ways to help you. At the end of the day, it's *your* career.

At the same time, don't seek out sponsors just because they look like you. I see women go out of their way to look for other women to sponsor them. My recommendation is to not fall into that trap. It represents a form of reverse unconscious bias where you feel like you need someone that looks like you to succeed.

Focus on the people that know you as a person and who can vouch for your work. The best sponsors are your immediate manager and your immediate manager's manager. If you collaborate with other teams, reach out to managers in other groups that you've interacted with. They have a vested interest in your career growth because if you've done a good job, your work has helped them accomplish their goals.

Earlier in my career, I worked in marketing at Microsoft. It was a phenomenal job that helped shape me into the executive that I am today. At the time, Microsoft was changing from selling traditional software to selling cloud based software. It was a momentous shift in the industry, and for Microsoft in particular.

When I was responsible for marketing our cloud offering in the U.S. at Microsoft, I already knew that my manager Angus and my skip-level manager Allison were my sponsors. I had great relationships with them. I knew exactly what my team and I were expected to deliver, how we were measured for success, and how our deliverables aligned to their goals. In addition, I built great rapport with Phil, the executive in charge of the broader cloud business for the U.S. market. Phil was a peer of Allison. I didn't report into Phil's organization, but I spent a lot of time working with him and his team to grow the cloud business. My job was to drive growth of this new category cloud product - in turn, he ensured to help me remove any roadblocks for the team and I to do that.

I never asked him to be my sponsor, in fact, I never asked any of my sponsors to be my sponsors per se. But I knew who was in my corner and who was putting my name forward for critical projects.

During that time, Microsoft was planning their annual internal Mid-Year Review (MYR). It was a business review of all business groups and geographic market clusters. The one for the US market was usually an all-day long event where the top 50 executives of the company discussed business performance and future plans for the company. It was held in a giant ballroom-turned conference room in a local hotel. Because I was working so closely with Phil on the cloud offering and was in charge of supporting him on the US cloud story for MYR, I got invited to come and be a fly on the wall at the MYR that year.

Sitting in the back of this giant conference room was a major learning opportunity for me and gave me the chance to hear the most senior management discussions on how they drive the company forward. I got to see how the leaders of one of the most successful companies in the world measured business performance, discussed future growth, and made decisions. I also learned how these senior executives handled tough questions. This MYR meeting and all the prep meetings leading up to it helped prepare me to be an executive one day.

As mentioned previously, Allison, who was my skip-level manager, while I was in the US cloud group, was also my sponsor. I had worked for her in another group earlier in my career at Microsoft. Shortly after she took on the new role to lead the US Marketing and Operations group, I decided I was ready for my next role and wanted to leave the team. I had been working in that team for about two years and felt it was time to move on. Because Allison and I had built a rapport from the previous team, I felt comfortable approaching her and telling her that I was looking for the next step in my career.

I have to digress a little to share a story with you on what NOT to do. I was ready to have a conversation with Allison about starting to search for a new role. Right after Allison delivered her first awesome All-Hands with our group, her spirits were high. I thought that was the best time to approach her, so I walked over and said "Allison, I'd love to find time to chat with you about my next role." She acknowledged my request and suggested we schedule a time.

When we met at the scheduled time, she said that she would like to give me some feedback first. She shared that she was feeling great at the All-Hands and it was a downer to hear one of her high potential leaders tell her about potentially leaving for a new role. I was dumbfounded and embarrassed that I didn't connect the dots on how poorly my timing actually was.

But I was glad that she was candid with me, and trust me, I would not make the same mistake twice. As karma would have it, I would be in the exact same situation years later, except this time I was the executive. Timing is everything.

Coming back to the sponsorship story, after Allison shared her feedback with me, she then said to me "I'd love for you to stay another year and take on an expanded role to drive the cloud business." She went on to say "I'll commit to you that by the second half of the year, I'll help you find your next role." We brainstormed roles that would be a good fit for me. In that process I became interested in an international assignment.

True to her word, during the second half of that year, she connected me with multiple executives that were either already working in another country or that had done an international assignment. I was eventually offered a Business Unit Lead role in Microsoft's China region, which was largely due to Allison's sponsorship. I didn't end up taking the role, but her advocacy was monumental in me even being considered for it.

THE THREE C'S

As an executive, when I looked for candidates to sponsor, I looked for three things: commitment, capacity, and competency.

I look for someone who's committed, meaning that they're committed to what they do and to the company. Commitment is key because that means the person will go the extra mile, and do what it takes to deliver positive outcomes.

The second trait I look for is their capacity. When I was getting my executive MBA, I made the conscious decision to put my career ambitions on the backburner - at least for the short term. I didn't have the capacity to do the work necessary to grow my career at that moment. My main focus was to balance my education and workload. I knew I would have the capacity to refocus on my career advancement after I graduated. It doesn't mean that I wouldn't be contributing to the company. You have to have the self-awareness to know when you have the capacity to focus on your career growth and when you don't.

The third trait I look at is competency. I want to sponsor someone who has the right skillset for what they do. Knowing that they have competency, knowing that they have capacity and a hunger to grow, and commitment is important. If you don't have the competencies yet, taking courses or volunteering to learn via stretch projects shows that you're aware of your areas for improvement and are actively focused on them.

Going back to Gail, when I met her, the first thing I noticed was her competency in digital marketing. Her results spoke for themselves. I knew she had the capacity to grow her career and was actively taking steps to increase her workload. Her work ethic and desire to learn and expand demonstrated her commitment to her profession and to the company. She was an ideal protégé and I was thrilled to sponsor her.

Lastly, assess your competencies and ask yourself if your current skill set will get you to the next level. Do you have the experiences to help you grow? Do you have a plan to help you acquire the skills and experiences that you need?

Early in my career I took multiple networking courses at the local college in Washington state. I wanted to be the best tech marketer I could be and knew I needed to understand technologies, so taking classes was a natural step. Classes and education help, but 70%, if not more, of your experience and training will come directly from your job. That's why I suggest volunteering for stretch projects, either within your department or with other teams. They'll give you valuable experiences and exposure to leaders of other teams. You'll build a reputation when you increase your competencies and demonstrate your commitment to helping other teams. Courses, training, and attending industry conferences are helpful, but there's nothing like acquiring new skills on the job. The skills and connections you gain are invaluable to recruiting sponsors that are willing to put their neck on the line to help advance your career.

Key Takeaways

- **Sponsorship Defined:** Sponsorship is the measurable partnership with a higher-level leader in an organization who exerts their political capital to help a high-potential protégé advance their career.
- **The "Frozen Middle":** Sponsorship helps professionals break out of the "frozen middle", the layer of middle management that many professionals, especially women and underrepresented minorities, get stuck in. Sponsorship enables companies to be proactive about their commitment to diversity.
- **Why Sponsorship Works:** Sponsorship helps protégés advance their careers and helps organizations intentionally build a diverse leadership pipeline. It enables influential executives to exert their influence and political capital to provide visibility, exposure, and access to opportunity to the protégés.
- **What Sponsors Look For:** To recruit an executive sponsor, you have to be on your game. They want to see mastery of your core competencies, a commitment to your profession, and have the capacity to take on more responsibility.
- **Sponsorship is the Bridge:** Sponsorship is the bridge to close the gap between your career North Star and your career roadmap (which I discuss in the next chapter)

3

BUILD YOUR CAREER ROADMAP

"All you need is the plan, the roadmap, and the courage to press on."

— EARL NIGHTINGALE

In chapter one, we discussed the importance of having a career North Star. In chapter two we discussed the transformational power of sponsorship. In this chapter, I want to help you put it together so you can use sponsorship to progress toward your career North Star.

To build your career roadmap, you need to take stock of your skillset, education, and experience. Your career roadmap will be informed by where you are in terms of the competencies you've built, the experience you have, and the education and training that supplement your on-the-job responsibilities. It will be guided by the career North Star you envisioned for yourself.

THINKING TWO JOBS AHEAD

There are many paths to reach your career North Star, but if you're early on in your career and only thinking about your next job, then you'll be looking at that role specifically for what it's worth. That's fine if you're just looking for new experiences and building competencies. But if you're on a mission, guided by your career North Star, you'll want to look beyond the face value of the current job and see it for its longer-term potential. That simple mindset shift serves as a lens by which to view the opportunities in front of you.

Practically speaking, I encourage people to think two jobs ahead. Ask yourself if the role(s) you're applying for will set you up for the next-next role that you ultimately want.

For example, I remember having a career development conversation with Jo on my team at Microsoft. Jo is a rare marketing talent who started her career as an engineer and made a pivot into marketing. She was ready for the next step in her career, so we were chatting about the job interviews she had thus far. She was hoping to get her first people manager job within the marketing function, but competition for people manager roles had always been fierce. I could tell that she was frustrated because after months of trying, she hadn't landed the role she wanted.

That said, she had gotten two internal offers; one was a senior marketing manager role as an individual contributor, and another was a people manager role in an engineering group. So I asked her, "Jo, where do you want to take your career longer term? What does your next-next role look like to you?" She told me that she saw herself going into general management. Therefore, developing people management skills was important to her at that point in her career. That was it! That was the clarity I wanted her to have for herself.

Because she was in marketing, she was fixated on finding a people management role within the marketing function. Knowing that her long-term goal was to be in general management, learning managerial skills was more important. With that clarity, she accepted the offer to lead a global engineering team. Thinking about medium-term career goals in that manner helps you break down the key elements you're looking for in your next role.

Over my career, I often came into direct competition with other candidates who had more experience than I did. It was eye-opening, exposing me to different aspects of the business. I learned just what I was up against and what skills I would need to acquire. I learned that depth of experience and a well-informed, outside perspective matters. In other cases, you may say you want to become a "specialist" in a certain function, and dive deep to become a subject matter expert. If you're thinking two jobs ahead of the job you're currently applying for, you can be deliberate and intentional in acquiring the skills and expertise that you need for your next roles.

Thinking two jobs ahead allows you to be more strategic and much more discerning in what position you take. If you happen to be in a position where you can't be as discerning (because you need a job NOW), you can make moves to acquire the skills and expertise to position yourself for your next job - the one you really want.

That's why I took that job as a junior buyer at ADIC when I couldn't get a marketing job after college. Not only did I *need* a job to pay rent and other essentials, I needed real-world experience. In that role, I built my credibility as a hard worker, an out-of-the-box thinker, and simultaneously took night classes at the University of Washington to learn computer networking and systems engineering. It all prepared me for the role I really wanted – a marketing job as a product manager in a tech company.

Later in my career as an executive, when I was deciding whether to leave Microsoft to go to Level 3 Communications, I had multiple opportunities in front of me. The job that I was seriously thinking about at that time was within Microsoft, the one that Allison, my skip-level manager helped connect me with. That job would have provided a chance to take my family and me to Beijing, China. It was the opportunity of a lifetime and that I had always wanted to do. I had always wanted to be on an international assignment, and I specifically wanted to go to China. Being that the Chinese economy was growing so fast in 2012, it was an incredible opportunity to make a name for myself at Microsoft in the high-growth Chinese market.

China was full of opportunity for me, both professionally as well as personally. For example, as a Chinese American from Hong Kong, I grew up speaking Cantonese but never learned Mandarin, which is the official language in mainland China. So not only was this a professional opportunity for me, but I would also have had the chance to learn Mandarin, which is something I personally wanted to do. A bigger reason was that my grandmother was still living in Hong Kong at that time. I visited her every year but I would jump at the chance to live closer to her. Needless to say, I was super excited about all of it.

Amid all this excitement and opportunity at Microsoft, I was presented with the chance to work for Level 3 Communications - completely out of the blue. It was at the time that they had just acquired Global Crossing (another large telecom company). That acquisition launched Level 3 into a Fortune 500 company and transformed them from a wholesale network services company to a direct-to-enterprise company. Level 3 used to sell networking technology, fiber optic infrastructure, and content delivery services to other small to large internet carriers. The Global Crossing acquisition initiated a massive pivot in their business model from being a wholesale company that sells to internet service providers to a company that sells directly to the enterprise market. It was a monumental shift in their business model from being a supplier to other companies, to being a direct seller. It's not dissimilar to the transition Costco made from being a wholesale company that supplied retail businesses to a direct-to-consumer company itself. It was a tall order and an ambitious business transformation, which was the reason they were looking for a new marketing executive with enterprise experience to help them reposition themselves in the market.

Initially, I declined the opportunity to interview for the Level 3 opportunity because I was far down in the path in the interview process for the China opportunity at Microsoft. Plus, I felt I had built strong credibility within the company already. But that process hit a speedbump when I was told that the offer process might take longer due to multiple approvals required for an international assignment. Given the uncertainty, I thought I should have a Plan B. So I spent a day in Broomfield, CO interviewing with the Level 3 executive team. By the end of the day, I was excited about the opportunity to be part of an executive team to transform the company.

By the time I was done with the Level 3 Interview process, I also received the good news on my offer for the Microsoft China opportunity. Now I had a problem to solve, a good problem it was. When I looked at both opportunities on their own, they both sounded amazing in their own way. If I could split myself in half and do both jobs, I would have. But life has its way of making you pick sides, so as hard as it was, I knew I had to decide and move on.

It was a tough career decision, but luckily, I had already decided on my career North Star and plotted my career roadmap, so I asked myself "Which one of these jobs will give me the best opportunity to ultimately become a Chief Marketing Officer one day?" In the Level 3 role, I would have reported directly to the Chief Marketing Officer. When I looked at it from that perspective, the decision was crystal clear. While I loved working at Microsoft and would have loved to stay, the Level 3 job would put me much closer to where I wanted to be for my career.

But I still didn't have the certainty I needed to pull the trigger.

Truth be told, it was a conversation I had with my previous boss Fred at Microsoft, a mentor and a sponsor of mine, that cemented my decision. Fred was the general manager who promoted me to a director at Microsoft, a significant hurdle to break through the "Frozen Middle" mentioned in the previous chapter and provided me ample opportunities and autonomy to take on big challenges and gave me visibility to some of the most senior executives in the company. So obviously his advice would mean a lot to me.

In my conversation with Fred, I shared with him the two incredible career opportunities, and I was clearly torn on which path to choose. He then said to me, "Maggie, this type of external opportunity [Level 3] is very rare. And if that doesn't work out, you have built strong credibility at Microsoft that you can always come back." That was it, that was the sage advice I needed to hear, and clarity in my mind of a "Plan B" if Plan A doesn't work out.

Another important plot of this story is that such career decisions are rarely a solo decision. We would have had to choose to relocate between Beijing, China and Boulder, Colorado. My husband JP and our four-legged kid Charlie were a big part of this family decision too. It was perfect timing that the company my husband worked for at that time had just been acquired by another company. He was ready to take a break from his 24x7 career as a chief technology officer and was very supportive of my career to be the lead for the family. As a smart partner, he opted out of providing input on which opportunity I should choose. Instead he said he'd be happy for us to move to either location.

This is a question I have gotten from women who are balancing between their own careers and their spouses. In my case, my husband's career was taking off faster than mine, so we had relocated twice for his career. Then my career was taking off and he gladly repaid the favors to follow my lead. Our decisions were always a joint one.

So, in the summer of 2012, JP, Charlie, and I embarked on a new adventure in Boulder, Colorado as I took on the role of Senior Vice President of Marketing at Level 3.

IT'S OK TO SAY NO

One of the things I hadn't really mastered during my corporate career was how to say "No". In business, you have to be clear about which markets and opportunities you'll prioritize and which you won't. It's equally important that you also declare what areas you won't compete in to safeguard the previous resources on key priorities. Specifying what you are not going to do is always harder because of the fear of missing out on opportunities you haven't foreseen yet. The same is true for your own career.

I've seen time and again, from my own personal experience, how important it is to say "No" when something doesn't feel right - or when I consider the opportunity cost on other priorities.

That's exactly what happened when I was at Microsoft leading the launch of a new category cloud product called Office 365 in the US market. It was a major bet for the company and was one of the most important launches I've ever worked on. The good news was that we were on track for our project. The team was working well together, and we were feeling good about the launch plan. During that time my skip level manager asked me, "Maggie, I would love for you to take on a stretch project, an important initiative for the company, to help launch Windows mobile." When I tell this story, I ask people "Have you heard of Windows Mobile?" And most of the time, no one raises their hand.

Microsoft had long been a juggernaut in desktop computing. Mobile computing was the next battleground. Apple had the iPhone all vertically integrated with its own iOS operating system, Google had the Nexus running Android. Microsoft wanted a piece of that pie. I was using a Windows Mobile phone running Microsoft operating system at that time, and it was actually pretty good. I loved the tiles on the home screens for your most frequently used apps. At the same time, I also knew that it's a very competitive market and the iPhone had the first mover advantage, a fiercely loyal fan base, and massive market share - so it would be an uphill battle to say the least. Windows Mobile at that time had a very low market share and I didn't personally feel that connected to the product. I was up for a big challenge, but this was going to be a stretch project for me, on top of the work I was already doing on the Office 365 launch.

It was a tough decision because my head was telling me to say "Yes" because I was honored that my executive thought of me for this opportunity and wanted me to take on this important project for the company. I also have this endless thirst to learn new things and take on big challenges. So naturally, I wanted to say yes. But at the same time, I'm also thinking to myself "If I say yes, am I truly the best person for this role?" I also worried about how working on this project would impact my work on my main focus, the Office 365 launch. I was responsible for making that a success in the US so if it flopped, it would fall on me.

I eventually mustered up the courage to tell my executive how much I appreciated that she tapped me for this project, but that I had to stay laser focused on the Office 365 launch and couldn't afford to take my eye off the ball. To my relief, she was very understanding, and they ended up finding a great person to take the role.

It's hard to say no to someone, especially those you respect, but at the end of the day, you also have to ask yourself "Does this align with what I want to do?" and "Can I do a great job?" If you can answer those questions, you'll know what action to take.

Ultimately, it was the right decision; not just for me personally, but for the company.

Saying "No" is hard. There's the fear of disappointing the other party. There's the fear of missing out on a potential opportunity. There's the fear of not looking like a team player. As hard as it is, if you make the decision with the other party in mind, it makes all the difference in the world.

In some cases, instead of saying "No", you may say "Not now" and explain how grateful you are for the opportunity and acknowledge your limitations. People respect you're self-aware enough to know what you can do, and what you can't. It's much better to be upfront and say "no" than it is to sheepishly take on a project that you know you can't deliver on.

This reminds me of a recent conversation I had with Jade, my cousin in Vancouver BC, Canada. She's like a little sister to me as I watched her grow from a baby to a responsible adult. Jade, a Millennial, is in her mid-thirties. She's also a wife and a mom with two young, adorable children under the age of five. She's been rising in her career as a vice president commercial interior designer. But between the COVID-19 pandemic, the heavy workload at work, and a family, she felt pretty burned out and was considering how best to bring more flexibility to her life. She has always dreamed of becoming an entrepreneur to start her own interior design business and felt that now was the best time to do so. In planning her exit from the company she worked at, she started to take on side projects to ease the transition to entrepreneurship without creating a financial burden for her family in the first year.

When I spoke with her, she told me that she's working even longer hours because she was getting more and more new clients for her side hustle. So I asked her why she was biting more than she could chew. She said, "If I turn an opportunity down, I worry that they may never return." That's the dilemma!

Sometimes we are so afraid of missing out that we rather shoulder more responsibilities and risk burning ourselves out than to say "No". So I said, "Instead of saying 'No', why don't you say 'Not now'. And if you know when you may have capacity, like in three months or six months, share that. It keeps the conversation going without losing an opportunity forever." Jade really liked that idea and has since then reached her career North Star to become her own boss. Because she has demonstrated her commitment and work ethics for all these years, her old boss has started a contract with her as one of her early clients in her new business.

KNOW YOUR NON-NEGOTIABLES

As we climb the corporate ladder, the stakes usually get higher and higher so we want to make the right career choices. This is not only important for your own career, but critical as you add other elements of your life you have to consider. I would get questions from executive women about how to decide which jobs to take and which ones not to take. I always suggest that it's important to have a short list of non-negotiables (emphasis on the word "short", keep it under three).

To that point, when I was one and a half years into my role at Level 3, I received a lot of calls from executive recruiters pitching different roles to me. I was happy in my role. I built strong relationships and credibility within the company for the marketing transformation. For the first time in the company's history, we were profitable. It was no easy task, considering there was a lot of legacy infrastructure, but the team was incredibly strong and focused.

On the personal side, JP, Charlie and I loved living in Boulder. We enjoyed taking Charlie for long walks in the park near our house, dining at our favorite restaurants (there were many!), and taking a summer drive to Estes Park, Rocky Mountain National Park, in our convertible. That said, I also knew that when I started feeling comfortable, it was time for something new. Knowing that I eventually wanted to be the CMO of a company, I identified three non-negotiables for my next role.

First, if I would say "Yes" to a role, it would have to be a company CMO role, not a specific business unit, not a regional CMO role, but a global CMO role for the entire company.

Second, it had to be in the software business. Having spent time in telecom, and previously spending time in software and hardware, the fast pace of innovations in the software industry is what I enjoyed most. So I was set on being in software.

The third one was a semi non-negotiable, and it had to do with geographical location. Most of the jobs would likely be outside of Colorado. If I were to move my family somewhere (again), it would have to be the Bay Area because I loved the energy, the tech scene, and the weather.

Those were my three non-negotiables and I looked at any opportunity that came across my desk from those filters. If a role didn't fit, I would pass on it. By having this focus, I prevented myself from being blinded by "shiny object syndrome". Any good executive recruiter will make a role sound exciting and sell you on how you're the perfect fit. For many executives, myself included, taking on big challenges drives us, so it's easy to be distracted by these stand-alone opportunities.

If I were to advise you, I'd say the following; when you think about the type of roles that you want to take next, think about your non-negotiables, along with your North Star. This is even more true for people who are mid-career or in an executive position. This is because the higher you go, the more likely you are to get visibility with recruiters. Recruiters will entice you with tempting roles. This same temptation applies to internal opportunities at your current company as well. When you do a good job, your reputation precedes you. People are more likely to reach out to you about potential next opportunities within the company.

It helps if you have a short list of things that you want to learn, or things that you specifically want to do. It gives clarity in figuring out the next role you want to take.

If you're early in your career, you may take on roles because they look fun to you. That's great. Your goal early in your career is to learn as many new things as possible so you get to know yourself. The higher you go in your career, the more selective you can be because of what you know about yourself and your non-negotiables.

Maybe your non-negotiables revolve around your values. Maybe they revolve around work/life balance. Maybe they revolve around emerging technologies or meaningful work. Maybe you value working from home. These are all important things to know. Have a shortlist, not a laundry list, of your non-negotiables.

Having a short list of non-negotiables will help you make strategic decisions that lead to the things that are important to you.

DECIDING YOU'VE LOST BEFORE YOU EVEN PLAY THE GAME

I love the saying, "You have to be where the puck is going to be, not where it is now." We do that in business all the time, predicting trends in the market, creating products to fill gaps in the market, generating demand for our current products, but why don't most people do that for their own careers?

If you're in product engineering, you think about product roadmaps. You think about where the market is going? You think about the technologies that are available to enable you to create products that would be the best for the market. It's the same thing when you think about sales. You think about your sales plan. You think about how you are going to penetrate market territories, and customer accounts. In marketing as well, you build your marketing plan. You think several years down the road on the brand you want to be known for.

Very rarely do people think about where they want to go in their careers. Rarely do I meet people who plan their careers like they would for a business.

I've also seen people going to the other end of an extreme. Since founding Tenshey, my leadership acceleration firm, I've worked with several women who painstakingly create detailed spreadsheets of the jobs they've applied to. They create a matrix of the skills and qualifications that the employer details in the job description, and then they check boxes in their spreadsheet where they feel they meet those qualifications. They look at the job descriptions to pinpoint the different skill sets employers are looking for and then assess themselves on how well they map to those requirements.

That level of detail and planning in general is awesome, but I've seen this backfire and work against them (more in that in a bit).

The first thing I say to them is that a job description is just a job description. Of course, you need to understand the requirements of the role and understand the skills and experiences that the hiring manager is looking for, but at the end of the day, you need to think about the kinds of problems you can help solve if you were hired. Rather than asking yourself "Do I tick all the boxes of what they're looking for?" you need to ask yourself, "How can I help the company solve their problems being in this role, regardless of whether I meet every single requirement in the job description?" You need to make sure that you meet the core competencies that the position needs and figure out how to apply your existing skills and experiences to achieve the outcome that they want.

For example, prior to going to Level 3, I never helped a company transition from a wholesale supplier to a direct seller nor had I worked in the telecom industry, but the experiences and skills that I accumulated throughout my career made me an ideal candidate for that job - a job that I ultimately got and excelled at. In fact, it's common for hiring managers to seek out candidates from different industries to broaden the perspectives of the team.

While it's important to look at the key competencies that the job description is calling for, don't try to map yourself to it 100%. Studies have shown that men go for jobs when they are only 60% qualified based on the available job description. On the other hand, women don't go for jobs until they feel that they're 90% to 100% qualified. This isn't just what I have witnessed countless times, the Harvard Business Review, Forbes, and The Economist have written at length about this phenomenon.

In other words, women are disqualifying themselves for jobs before even applying! It's like quitting a game before it starts because you've already decided that you're going to lose, and it's downright sad to see. I'm struck by how many smart, ambitious, tenacious women have sat on the sidelines because they thought that they weren't good enough to even apply for a role.

My advice is to explore, to experiment, and to give yourself a chance to do something you want to do. That means giving yourself the chance to succeed AND to fail. But never disqualify yourself from an opportunity.

When it comes to your career North Star, you have to get into the game. Go ahead, put your hat in the ring. Take those risks and become comfortable with the outcome, no matter what happens. The worst thing that could happen is that they say "*no.*"

A COACH IS YOUR SECRET WEAPON

As you navigate the journey to reach your career North Star, you'll need a confidant, a sounding board to help you do what you need to do to get there - speaking from experience, having a coach was a secret weapon of mine to help get me where I wanted to be.

I met my coach, Mary, back in 2011 when I was at Microsoft. My group just hired a new General Manager to replace Fred, who was taking on a new role in the Business Applications business. It was bittersweet; as mentioned previously, Fred was a great manager, a sponsor, and a mentor to me. I had tremendous autonomy and visibility under his leadership. He helped me accelerate my career growth at Microsoft, and most of all, it was fun working on his team.

I was happy for Fred. At the same time, I was anxious to see how this new executive was going to manage the team. The thought that kept playing out in my mind was "*How is this going to change my role?*"

I was speaking to one of my mentors at the time about my angst and she said, "You know what, I think having an executive coach would really help you in navigating this transition." At that point, I didn't know what an executive coach did, but my mentor told me that I should talk to her coach, Mary, so I said, "Okay, great, I'll talk to her."

I had a conversation with Mary, and instantly felt like we had good chemistry. She asked me challenging questions like "Where do you want to go in your career? Where do you feel like you're at in relation to your career goals?" One question she asked that really got me to pause was, "Maggie, what would you like to do or accomplish during your lifetime both personally and professionally in order to consider your life well lived?" What a powerful question!

After that brief time I spent with her, I felt rejuvenated in my career focus. I went to my new boss and said, "Hey, Angus, I had a great discussion with Mary, an executive coach whom my mentor (his peer) recommended. Is it okay that I work with Mary as my coach?" He was incredibly open to it and enthusiastically supported me doing that. His willingness to support me allayed my fears and assuaged some of the trepidation I had around the transition to this new manager. "We're going to get along just fine" I thought to myself.

At that time, I was tagged as a high potential talent within Microsoft, a factor that certainly made it easier for me to get a coach, covered by the company as a leadership development cost.

One of the myths that we hear, not as much today, but more so back in the days, is, "Only people who are in trouble, or who are having performance issues would ever need a coach." But when you're a high performer, having a coach helps you unlock your potential for accelerated growth and paves the path to a leadership position in the future. It enables you to be a better leader for your team and the company. From that perspective, it's tremendously helpful to have a coach.

A coach is like a secret weapon in your career. Luckily for me, Microsoft was willing to pay for it, and so did my subsequent employers. I believe in coaching so much that I incorporated executive coaching as a development tool for my teams to unlock their own potential.

I found so much value in working with Mary that I continued working with her when I went to Level 3, when I went to SAP, and when I founded Tenshey for women and minority leaders. Mary is still my personal executive coach that not only helps me, but my clients as well. She has helped me make massive shifts in my mindset, my career, and my business - giving me the courage and clarity to make bold moves despite hesitation or self-doubt. She's helped me remove my blind spots as a leader as well.

It's hard to put a price tag on that.

Coaching services can be expensive, especially if you were to pay for it out of pocket. That said, many companies, from startups to enterprises, have set aside development funds for employees. For most of my jobs, I didn't have to pay out of pocket. At Microsoft, my manager supported me to have a coach as part of my leadership development. As a senior executive at Level 3 and SAP, it was part of my compensation negotiation.

The purpose of coaching is to ultimately help me be a more dynamic, high-performing leader, so my employers were willing to invest in it. I believe wholeheartedly in the power of executive coaching, and I suggest that you approach your manager to cover the investment. Oftentimes they can tap into a talent development or continuing education budget so you don't have to pay out of pocket.

If you're starting a new position, especially as an executive, you can ask for a coaching and development stipend as part of your compensation negotiations. Whatever stage you're at, it's a conversation worth having with your manager and your human resources department. Not every company will pay for it, but one thing we do with our clients at Tenshey is help them have that conversation with their employer. We've developed a manager conversation guide to help have that conversation with their managers.

Here are some talking points in our manager conversation guide that may be useful to you for your discussion.

- *Coaching benefits to me as a leader for [company name]*
- *Stronger self-awareness on my leadership capabilities which leads to actions for development*
- *Better align my personal values to my contribution to [company name]*
- *Coaching benefits to [company name] and my workgroup*
- *Strengthening myself for more adaptive thinking in our complex and fast-paced environment*
- *Cultivating a coaching culture resulted in stronger team collaborations*

In chapter 2, I shared with you the differences between a mentor, a coach and a sponsor. I mentioned that my mentor was the person who convinced me to hire Mary as my coach. This is a good example to differentiate the roles a mentor and a coach play. A mentor is someone who has "been there and done that" along the path that you want to be on. A mentor may also be a person who has excelled in a skill area that you want to learn about. Another way of saying is that mentors are the ones that have that expertise you want to emulate or to learn already.

For example, at that time, my mentor was a General Manager at Microsoft over a broader group that I was part of. She had climbed the ladder and understood some of the challenges and the opportunities that someone like me would face. Since I was a mid-career professional, she served as a model to help me go down the trail that she had already blazed. I learned a lot from her experience and her business acumen, and bounce ideas off of her for situations that I was in.

On the other hand, as my coach, Mary acted as a confidant to me. It's like she held a mirror in front of me to hold me accountable to the goals and development I set for myself. The things that we talked about revolved around self-awareness, team dynamics, leadership traits, and how to navigate some specific sticky leadership scenarios.

She also helped develop me as a leader by assessing my strengths, my motivations, and blind spots as a leader. She helped me crystalize my plan to foster a high-performance team in this fast-changing tech world I was in.

Mary would also hold me accountable to those actionable plans, to help me to continue to progress in my career. And in her own way, she gently nudged me when my imposter syndrome presented itself. She helped me identify blind spots and pushed me out of my comfort zone (boy did she push me out of my comfort zone and hold me accountable!)

Back at Microsoft, I was presented with the opportunity of a lifetime; I had the opportunity to interview the CEO at the time, Steve Ballmer, at our Global Women Leadership Summit. The way it occurred still amazes me to this day.

At the time, I was part of a small group of employees that was invited to the Working Mother Media conference at Microsoft in New York. There was a group of seven or eight of us waiting to board our flight back to Seattle after the conference, so we got into a small discussion. I don't remember the details of what we even talked about, all I remember was that it was a nice, friendly chat among colleagues at the airport – or so I thought.

A month or so later, I was about to go on stage to participate in a panel discussion at a Microsoft partner event and my mobile phone rang. The voice on the other end of the line said, "Maggie, this is Gwen Houston, the Chief Diversity and Inclusion Officer at Microsoft, we met at the WMM conference a few months ago and I was wondering if you'd be willing to moderate a session interviewing Steve Ballmer at the upcoming Global Women Leadership Summit". I couldn't believe what I had just heard. *"Steve Ballmer!"* I thought to myself.

My immediate reaction was *"HELL yeah!"*, though I know my response to Gwen was a bit more eloquent than that. Once my excitement subsided, I asked "Why me?" She went on to say "I was really impressed by what you said and how you carried yourself during our chat at the airport. You asked great questions. I then checked out your talent profile and thought you would be a great fit."

The Global Women Leadership Summit would take place in front of thousands of employees at the Microsoft Conference Center on campus in Redmond Washington, and simultaneously live streamed across the world for our employees in other locations. I was going to be sitting on stage with Steve and talking for an hour, covering a wide range of topics from Microsoft's strategic priorities to his perspective on emerging technology trends in the market, and of course, the importance of diversity and inclusion.

I didn't remember the story so well, but Mary sure did! She recounted the story of me telling her how excited I was to interview Steve Ballmer. At the same time, I was really, really nervous. "What if the interview was a flop? What if I make a fool of myself in front of thousands, maybe tens of thousands, of Microsoft employees?" I thought. I was absolutely petrified.

In the midst of all that emotion, Mary calmly asked me, "Maggie, what's the worst thing that can happen? Sure, you might flop and look stupid. Is that an outcome that you can live with?" It was such a powerful question, one that she's asked me time and again when I come to her about a situation that I'm unsure of.

That simple question almost always results in an enthusiastic "Yes, I CAN live with the outcome of this failing considering the risk and benefits equation. There's so much reward if things go right, that this little bit of risk won't deter me from taking action." When I looked at the risks and benefits, the benefits overwhelmingly outweighed the risk of looking stupid. Truth be told, for something with such importance, I know I would go above and beyond in my preparation to minimize the probability of a bad outcome. I did all my prep and conducted that interview with a ton of enthusiasm and excitement. As it turns out, it went really, really well.

To this very day, anytime I feel self-doubt or fear, I can hear Mary's voice in my head asking "Okay, Maggie, let's say you do this, what's the worst thing that can happen? What are you afraid of? And if that happened, would it really be the worst thing in the world?" Having that conversation, even if it's a fictional conversation in my head, helps me feel a lot more confident and make bold, decisive moves.

After that presentation with Steve Ballmer, I got so many text messages, emails, and high-fives from people saying, "Maggie, that was amazing!" It was a memorable moment in my career - not only because of the recognition I gained, but because of the confidence I developed.

That comes back to the value of having a coach who helps you unlock your own limiting beliefs. We can be our own worst critics, and as you've seen earlier, it's a proven fact that women talk themselves out of job opportunities because of their own limiting beliefs. In fact, I've seen women talk themselves out of even applying for a job because they don't think they're good enough. A good coach can help you step outside of your fears and unlock your potential.

Whenever you're faced with a nerve-racking decision, step back and ask yourself the question "If you do this and it doesn't go the way you want, what's the worst thing that can happen? And can you live with that result? Better yet, what can you do to mitigate some or all of the risks?" If that is something that can happen, then you have your answer on whether you want to proceed or not.

In general, whenever you're faced with a big decision and are afraid to move forward, ask yourself if taking this action will help you get to your career North Star. If so, and you see that the downside risk is relatively small or manageable, then jump into it wholeheartedly and do it.

At the same time, it won't always be so black and white. If you remember earlier when I talked about taking the road less travelled, not every single decision you make must align with your career North Star. There are so many decisions in your day-to-day life, including your personal life, that affect which move you need to make. The point is to not let fear inhibit you from taking an action that you really want to take. A coach will talk you through those scenarios and help you rethink your fears.

As successful as that event was, there was *one* lesson I learned what not to do. I was excited and felt honored to have had the privilege of interviewing the CEO of Microsoft. I was thrilled at the opportunity and recognition I received within Microsoft, but later that day, I bumped into a mentor of mine in the office hallway. She congratulated me and then proceeded to say, "Maggie, some people are talking, wondering why you got to interview Steve at the event. You may want to tone down your excitement." My heart dropped. I was thinking, did I do something that I shouldn't have? I didn't know how to react to the advice, but I acknowledged it.

My mental note of this experience came back to me when I was an executive at Level 3. When one of the talented marketers told me that she wanted to quit a stretch project working closely with me. She was working closely with me and other executives and was in the limelight because of it. She told me that she wanted to quit because people were whispering amongst themselves, wondering how she got chosen for this stretch project.

What people were really wondering was "Why wasn't it me?" So I told her that she was chosen for the project because of her experience and work ethic. She earned it, and that it would be a missed opportunity if she dropped the project. Then I saw a big smile on her face, and she went on to deliver the project with great impact. Even years later, whenever I spoke with her, she shared the fond memory she had of the project.

Women and underrepresented minorities have enough self-doubts as we climb the ladder. Being an ally and celebrating their success along the way seem more appropriate to me.

As an Asian American woman who also looks young for my age, it's not unusual that I would hear whispers like "Did she get the job (or opportunity) because she's a woman or because she's a minority?" These whispers also implied that I did not earn these opportunities with merits because I don't look like most executives, majority white and male.

My advice for other women and minority leaders who have similar experiences is to tune out the noise. Let your results and impact speak for you. When you can show the impact you make on the project or a role, the noise will die down.

YOUR SUPPORT SYSTEM

I can't emphasize enough how important your support system is. No one can do this alone. When you think about your career, it's a marathon, not a sprint. And just like having friends, family, and fans all along the path of a marathon keeps you going, you need a strong support system as you run the marathon of your career.

For me, my support system consisted of my family, my friends, my managers, my colleagues, my mentors, my coach, and my sponsors. All of these folks played a vital role in helping me achieve my career goals.

As mentioned previously, my husband and I have moved four times as we pursued our professional interests, twice for my husband's job, and twice for mine. We had to think about how we could support each other and our career aspirations along the way. For example, when I was doing my executive MBA program, I decided to also take on a brand-new role within Microsoft. It was a tough decision that affected us both, so my husband and I talked about it. We talked about how he probably wasn't going to see a whole lot of me because I would either be at work, doing school projects, or going to class.

Those are the things that clear communication will help, even when some conversations may be tougher than others. Those are the types of things you'll need to communicate with your support system. But you'll need to communicate what you need from your support system – no one will read your mind. They're there to support you, cheer for you, and pick you up when you fall, but you need to tell them what you need from them.

RECRUITING YOUR SUPPORT SYSTEM

As far as building a support system goes, my advice is to recruit your board of advisors early on in your career. Some people like to have a more formal board of advisors, while I personally prefer things to stay fluid and flexible. Think about the characteristics you need in your board of advisors. I've found that I worked well with people that knew me as a person. It was usually my long-time friends because they knew me long before I became an executive. College roommates and colleagues from the early days of my career who knew me before I took on big roles were my support system. As I rode the ups and downs in my career and in my personal life, I knew that I could always count on them as an honest sounding board for me.

At the same time, as you take on different roles within your company or even at a different company, you'll need different people with a broader set of experiences as well. You'll need mentors familiar with the scenario you're in. You'll need peers who can be mentors to you, especially when you're trying to learn about the culture and the unspoken subculture that governs how decisions are made. You'll need your managers and sponsors to help you to continue to grow your skills. So your support system is a combination of people based on the scenario that you're in.

As far as building your initial support system, like mentors, when you're in a new environment such as a new group or a new company, I find it best done organically. Most of the time, you'll attract mentors because they see someone who has potential and who will naturally want to help you. I've found that the best way to attract mentors is by showcasing your will and your appetite to learn.

When I think of myself as a mentor, and when I look back at the mentors I've had in my career, they were never looking for anything in return. They wanted to help ambitious people and next generation leaders to achieve their potential. They wanted to use their own experience, knowledge, and skills to help advance someone else that demonstrated drive and a will to succeed. They want nothing from you other than to see you succeed.

The simplest way to engage someone for a mentorship conversation is to ask if you can get 30 minutes of their time to pick their brain on a specific topic. For those you can meet in person, I always ask if I can buy them a coffee and pick their brain. I don't think I have ever gotten a "No", but some meetings may take longer to get on the calendar due to busy schedules.

As far as recruiting your managers and sponsors to help you advance your career, you need to align your goals with their goals. This should be relatively natural because your business goals should already align with your managers anyway. If not, that should be ironed out first. It's also basic human interaction, if you want something from someone, I always believe that it's best you figure out how you can help them first.

You attract sponsors and managers to your board of advisors by demonstrating that you're working towards the same goals that they are. Since you're supporting them in their business objectives, they'll naturally want to support you with your goals. Again, it's predicated on you helping the business, so it's in their best interest to help you as well.

PUTTING IT IN PRACTICE

When you think about a sponsor relationship, it goes without saying that your goal is to grow your career. The difference is that you're asking for your executive to give you visibility, access to their network, and advocacy – so it's imperative that you can put them in the best light possible.

One of the most common misconceptions in the workplace is that moms, especially moms with young children, are not dedicated to career growth. That cannot be further from the truth. Of course, there are cases where women who are mothers choose to take a step back on their career until their children reach a certain age to re-focus on their career growth, however, I have met mothers who are just as dedicated to their career as to their family. They may be the breadwinner for their families and they also have ambitious professional goals. Many of the career-oriented moms I have worked with developed a very strong support system that helps with their personal and family responsibilities so they can also integrate a successful career.

So when you think about your capacity for career growth, look at where you are in your life and decide if you have the capacity to dedicate to your career growth. Remember, there are no right or wrong answers.

I've had debated leaders, usually male leaders, who had already counted some women, who also happened to be mothers, out for new roles or opportunities because they perceived them as not as dedicated to their careers. I would suggest to the leaders to focus on the role at hand, and ask questions about how they would handle the workload or in some cases business travels if they were given the role.

Sometimes you'll find yourself at capacity, but can't afford to take a break from your career. If you want to advance your career but are at the limits of your capacity, it's time to engage your support system or explore outsourcing help where possible.

Your support system will be a key part of your growth, regardless of what stage you're at in your career. In addition to providing the emotional support you need, they'll often pitch in with physical support if that's what you need.

For example, I met Asha George when she was just promoted to a Vice President at Dell Technologies. I was not only honored to witness Asha's growth as an executive, but our two teams got to work together to co-create Dell's Diversity Leadership Accelerator Program to propel more women into leadership through sponsorship. I have always been impressed by Asha's drive and creativity in finding ways to solve big challenges. She has since then become the Chief Diversity, Equity and Inclusion Officer at Electronic Arts. Over the past few years, I got to know Asha better. Asha has a young family and a demanding job. When she was at Dell, her business travels would take up 50% to 60% of the time. Her husband was also an executive at another large tech company and spent 50% of his time travelling. Their combined schedules made raising a family very difficult, but her support system helped them balance their personal and professional commitments.

She told me how she relied on her parents and in-laws for support at home. They helped feed the kids, take them to school, and pick them up from sports events as needed. She and her husband, both thriving in their corporate careers, wouldn't have been able to advance in their careers without the strong support from their family.

Asha explained, "It really takes a village. I joke around with other moms who ask 'How do you do the mom thing?'" With both Asha and her husband on the road half the time for their jobs, raising a family takes creativity and compassion. She said, "If I see a neighbor's kid at the bus stop and it's pouring rain I tell them 'Call your mom, you're coming with me.' and I take all of those kids to school. Their parents know if 'Miss Asha' asks, they can go. At the same time I know, if I'm stuck on a call or at an airport somewhere, I can simply send a text and I know I have an army of people that will jump in to help."

She understands the power of "paying it forward" and being a good neighbor to others – literally and figuratively. "If you're a good neighbor, people will naturally come to help you. It's not because I expect anything, it's because they know that you'll do good for them."

She elaborated how she also relies on her parents, in-laws, and nanny to provide a sense of structure and familiarity for her kids when she and her husband are working, "We have someone that helps [with the kids]. I also have very active in-laws and parents that jump in and help. They're able to maintain a routine in the house. That way I can go to work in peace."

The next thing she said demonstrated a deep sense of self-awareness, and honestly caught me by surprise. She went on to say, "That is a place of privilege, not everybody gets that." There are plenty of single mothers in the workforce that can't afford domestic help. The point is that it's almost impossible to balance a demanding career and busy home-life without support. As cliche as it sounds, it does take a village, so lean on friends, family, neighbors as much as you can.

Her parting advice was "Build your personal board of directors. When you get to the top, you need your support system. You need to surround yourself with those people."

FIRST THINGS FIRST - YOUR BIG ROCKS

Stephen Covey, the author of the classic "The Seven Habits of Highly Effective People" originally published in 1989, gave a popular demonstration of his concept of "Big Rocks". You can watch the video on YouTube if you aren't familiar with it, but the gist is that you can't fit everything in your life and do it well; building career, raising a family, health, volunteering and giving back, professional development, on top of the thousands of other little tasks, the "pebbles", that nag on you week after week. Trying to do everything and be everything at the same time is a recipe for frustration, disappointment, and burnout.

In today's workplace given how digitally we're connected, it is not unusual to see people feel like they have to be "on" twenty-four hours a day, seven days a week. When your work colleagues can email, text, or Slack you 24x7, it's hard to escape. As a result, you end up getting sucked in doing tons of little things, the "pebbles".

What I took away from Stephen Covey's "Big Rocks" talk is that you have to figure out the "big rocks" in your life that are most important to you; the pillars upon which you build your life, the axis that your life revolves around.

What are the things that are most important to you? Who are the people and the relationships that are most precious to you? We tend to always say, "My family is very important. Family comes first." but when you look at how much of your time or how present you were when you spend the time on what you call your personal priorities, that may not be in congruence with your words.

Protecting what's important to you (your Big Rocks), whether it's family, or your career, or your health, or volunteering, necessitates taking steps to actively protect them so that other competing priorities don't erode the time that you're supposed to dedicate to them.

For me, especially when I was a corporate executive with a grueling work and travel schedule, I had to protect my family time on Saturdays, annual vacations, and tennis. Tennis is how I unplug and stay semi-healthy, so I vigorously guarded that time. When I wasn't traveling for work, I would always protect my Monday night and reserve it for playing tennis as opposed to attending yet another industry event or working away on my computer. I literally block it on my calendar and would suggest you do the same. I have spoken with people who said they tried to block their calendar but that didn't work. When I peeled back the onion, the part that didn't work was that they never "acted" on it. When people try to schedule a meeting during their "blocked time", they oblige without hesitation. Of course that didn't work. If that time is sacred, you have to let the other parties know so they find another time that works for you. There will be times that you couldn't avoid, but hopefully that is an exception rather than the norm. Figure out what's important to you and block it on your calendar (and mean it) so that no one takes that time away.

When I manage teams, I always ask people, "What motivates you? What's important to you?" Knowing that can also help me to help them protect their time so that they can focus on what's important to them. It could be a parent saying that their kids are on a soccer team, and they go to practice at 3pm every Wednesday. I would ask them to block out those times so that people avoid scheduling meetings with that person during that time. Doing that means a lot to people and is a great way to build a strong relationship with your team so that they feel cared for. This not only helps prevent burnout, but it also shows that you care about their well-being, ultimately increasing their sense of belonging to the team and organization.

Key Takeaways

- **Think Two Jobs Ahead**: Treat your career like you would a tech product by creating a roadmap. Don't just think about the job in front of you, prepare yourself for your next-next job.
- **It's Ok to Say "No"**: It's ok to say "No" when you feel an opportunity isn't a good fit for you. Saying "Not now" is an effective way to politely say "No" while preserving for a better time in the future.
- **Find a Coach**: A coach is your secret weapon. Your coach can help you step out of your limiting beliefs and step into your power. Many companies will even pay for a coach if you can show how it will improve your performance.
- **Build Your Support System**: Success doesn't happen alone. Build a strong support system of friends, family, mentors, coaches, and sponsors that care about your success. They'll celebrate your

successes and will be there for you when things are tough.

- **Identify Your Big Rocks**: What do you care about in your life? Figure out what's important to you personally and professionally and build your life around them.

Here's a Tenshey Career Roadmap framework you can use.

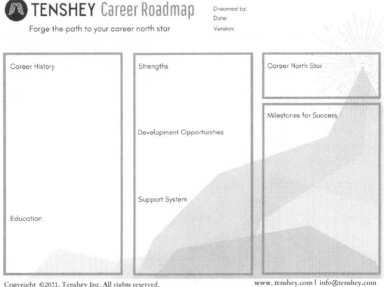

TENSHEY Career Roadmap

Forge the path to your career north star

Dreamed by:
Date:
Version:

Career History

Education

Strengths

Development Opportunities

Support System

Career North Star

Milestones for Success

www. tenshey.com | info@tenshey.com

4

ACTIVATING YOUR LEADERSHIP JOURNEY

"Without initiative, leaders are simply workers in leadership positions."

— *BO BENNETT*

This chapter is about taking steps to implement your leadership journey in your career roadmap; the competencies you need to build, the experiences you need to gain, and ultimately culminating in this roadmap template that you've created. We'll go over the steps you need to take as well as the lessons I learned along my own journey.

BUILDING YOUR AUTHENTIC LEADERSHIP VOICE

Think about the next steps that you need to take, where you've been, and where you want to be. Now ask yourself what new competencies you need to build in order to get to your career North Star? Now that you have a rough idea of the steps, you need to think of the actions you need to take to get there.

When we think about building your authentic leadership voice, it's about getting to know who you are and projecting that persona externally. Along your journey, you start to get to know yourself better and start thinking about your growth opportunities. Knowing the kind of leader you are, or want to be, will help prepare you for those opportunities.

A question I get often is "Can I be a leader even if I don't manage people?" To that I say, "Yes, absolutely!" Leadership qualities can be learned as early as childhood. As a kid, I grew up with my three younger cousins. We played together every weekend when our extended family got together. As the eldest of four, I was taught early on that I needed to lead by example. This concept applies to the workplace as well. Even in my first role as a junior buyer, I led projects that involved cross-functional teams. When we think about building your authentic leadership voice, it's about getting to know who you are, how you work with others and how you would like others to work with you.

You have to think of these opportunities in terms of what excites you and the kind of leader that you need to become if you want to succeed in those roles.

That brings me to the story of my manager Dan back at Microsoft. Dan was great with people; he invested in getting to know each of his team members and was hands-on in helping them be successful. Everyone just loved Dan, both as a person and as a leader - including me. He knew his leadership style and embraced it.

As I was cultivating my own leadership voice, I loved the outcomes Dan achieved as a people manager. At the same time, I also knew that I was not Dan. Our communication and leadership styles were very different, neither was right or wrong, just different.

During that time, our group had all completed the Insights Discovery Leadership assessment to learn about our own styles as well as how best to work with others. In addition to using adjectives to describe each of the personality types, it uses different colors to accentuate each style, from Cool Blue, to Fiery Red, Sunshine Yellow, and Earth Green. Dan's style is categorized as "Sunshine Yellow". He was sociable, dynamic, demonstrative, enthusiastic, and persuasive. My style was categorized as "Fiery Red". I'm competitive, demanding, determined, strong-willed, and purposeful.

I realized that to stay true to who I am as a person and as a leader, I need to attract people who not only share the vision of what I do, but the "how" as well. I'm not the high-EQ person that Dan is. At the same time, I would pride myself that people who work with me typically know where they stand with me. I always like people on my team to know who I am as a leader, my leadership principles and my communication style, so they know what to expect from me - and what I expect from them. I want them to know where they stand with me in terms of their role, the projects they're working on, and where they want to go in their career. The reputation that I've developed as a leader is that I'm demanding but fair.

They know that I care about them and want to help them in their career, but I always tell them "If you don't want to be on a championship team, then you don't want to be on my team, because that's what my team is all about." It's direct and honest, and that's who I am. I believe in setting expectations and want to make sure that the other party knows what they're getting themselves into so they can decide whether my management style works for them.

For instance, when I interview and hire talent for my teams, I like to paint a picture of how difficult the role will be. I don't sugarcoat anything because the people who want to take the job are the ones that really want the big challenges. They want things to be hard, they want to get to that impossible place, and they want to hit those big goals for the business.

As I grew as a leader, I went from "I wish I could be more like Dan" to "This is who I am as a leader, and I own it". Knowing yourself and who you are as a leader, even if you aren't in a leadership role yet, will serve you and your team well in the future.

Throughout my career, and now in my own business, everyone that I've ever hired has been inspired by the vision of where we want to be and drawn to the big challenges. I'd go as far as to say that they've craved challenges and wanted to play at a higher level. They embraced doing hard things and thrived because they knew what they signed up for.

TUNING OUT THE NOISE

At Tenshey, a persistent area women tell us that they need help with is building their confidence. I've mentioned the importance of tuning out the noise from external sources, but this applies to the noise within us as well.

That means tuning out your inner critic; you know, the little voice in the back of your head that tells you "You aren't good enough." It's a subtle voice that drains your self-confidence and makes blazing your path a daily struggle. It feeds into the sense of impostor syndrome that many of us feel and erodes the executive presence we need to show up powerfully and dynamically in our roles.

Imposter syndrome is a real phenomenon and has a major impact on your performance. Imposter syndrome is loosely defined as the persistent belief you don't deserve your success and that at any given moment, you may be exposed as a fraud.

I recently started mentoring an executive who is the Head of People function within a company. I've seen her present in executive meetings where I could see her discomfort through the video conferencing screen. While she mastered the functional skills of her job, the "people" side of her presentation did not match the expertise she certainly has on the topic.

In our first mentoring conversation, she asked me whether I had experienced imposter syndrome in my career. I said "all the time" but that I may be better at hiding it than some. I tackle business challenges by breaking them down into manageable chunks. When I doubt myself, I ask, "What are the factors that are causing me to doubt myself?" and "What can I do to solve them?"

Going back to the scenario she was going through; she knew she had strong expertise in the HR function. She doubted herself because she didn't know the attendees at her meetings. To make matters worse, they were all virtual, so she hadn't met a majority of them and had no rapport with them. As a result, she didn't have a firm grasp of what was expected of her. I also discovered that she had not developed a habit of crystalizing the story she was planning to tell prior to her presentations. Instead, she's been relying on her PowerPoint slides to guide her, which made her sound scripted and uncertain of herself.

Here's the advice I shared with her on preparing for an important executive or board meeting:

1. **Invest the time to connect one-on-one with key stakeholders** before the actual meeting. By doing so, not only are you able to get their early feedback, you'll be able to find out who will be your allies in the meeting as well as those you may be getting push back from. They'll feel less intimidating to you since you've already built rapport with them.

2. **Hone in on the story you'd like to tell.** Too often, I have seen people rely too much on their PowerPoint slides to tell their stories, instead of the other way around. Those slides are meant to supplement the key points you want to make. You want to identify the main points you're trying to make up front and use your slides to accentuate your points.

3. **Anticipate the type of questions and feedback you'll get from the participants** and how you'd handle objections and challenging questions.

4. **Practice, practice, practice.** We'll go into more details on this but rehearsing your pitch even in front of a mirror or with a few colleagues will boost your confidence when you're in the actual meeting.

Armed with those tips, she can now show up to a meeting with poise and quiet self-assurance. At the end of the day, there's no substitute for planning, preparation, and practice. Overtime, you'll develop an "executive presence" that others can sense.

The number one thing we see people wanting to work on with our coaches is how they can expand growth in their career. The second thing is how they can build more confidence. Third is, how do they build executive presence?

Executive presence is a bit of a loaded term. You can't easily put your finger on and say, "If I do X, Y, and Z, that means I have my executive presence" because it's about perception. In this case, executive presence is the perception that *others* have of you.

To me, someone with a strong executive presence is someone that has confidence in who they are as a leader and in what they know. They're confident in their domain of expertise. They walk into a room knowing their stuff, and can command a room because of their credibility. To me, that comes back down to knowing and being comfortable with who you are and putting in the work to be on top of your game.

We all have a little voice in the back of our heads telling us that we aren't good enough. It still plays in my head from time to time, but I've learned to drown it out. If you commit to planning, preparation, and practice you'll more likely be able to drown it out as well.

"Tuning out the noise", whether it be from your inner voice, or outside influences, is so important. It will sabotage you and block you from achieving your potential - if you allow it to.

Coming back to imposter syndrome, what we see, especially in the tech industry and other male-dominated industries like oil and gas or financial services, is that day in and day out, you are working in an environment where you may be the only woman, or one of the few women, in the room.

Sometimes you'll feel like you can't speak up and make your voice heard, and in a lot of cases, you may begin to think, "Maybe I'm not good enough for this job. Maybe I'm not good enough for this opportunity." It's a vicious cycle because once you start thinking that, it becomes a self-fulfilling prophecy.

You don't raise your hand. You don't speak up. You don't apply for the job. You don't ask for that big promotion. All because you don't think you "deserve" it until you're 100% ready. You combat that by building confidence and taking it one step at a time.

Let's say you're giving a presentation to an executive, the #1 one thing I suggest is to make sure you know your topic. Whatever topic you're talking about, present yourself as the domain expert. You need to know it so well that people can't help but respect you. At the same time, you need to be able to explain it so well that even a five-year-old could understand it.

The issue I see is people build up this domain expertise, but they get so excited about what they know, or they want to make such a strong impression, that they forget to deliver the information in a way that the other party can digest it. You need to remember that the executive(s) you're presenting to may not be as close to the subject as you are, or may not be familiar with the subject at all. The ability to succinctly share what you're trying to communicate and share actionable insights that help executives make informed decisions will set you apart and develop a reputation for yourself.

I can't overstate the importance of practice to boost confidence and combat impostor syndrome. Whenever I have an executive presentation, I always do a dry run. In fact, experts in nearly every profession in the world - from elite athletes, to pilots, to salespeople, to public speakers - all spend time rehearsing where they practice over and over again in private, so that they get every detail right. Pilots spend hours and hours in flight simulators. Elite tennis players spend hours practicing a specific shot. The power of importance of dry runs simply can't be understated.

In your case, whether you want to dry-run in front of a mirror or dry-run with a few colleagues, ask people to challenge you with questions that help you think about what things that you may be missing. You'll feel more confident going into that discussion, because you've already thought through questions and objections, which makes you come across as well prepared and on top of your materials.

That said, it's a known fact that despite being prepared, and despite being on top of your game, women generally have it harder than most men. Why? Because men are already accepted as part of the in-crowd. Most people expect to see men in management. According to a report published in 2020, just 6% of S&P 500 companies have a woman CEO. There were 40 CEOs named Michael or James compared to 31 women CEOs; and there were more chairs of the board named John than women chairs leading their board of directors. Women start at a disadvantage so they have to work harder than a man to prove themselves.

If you're a woman of color, it's even more challenging. Now think about if you're someone for whom English is a second language, or an ethnic minority, or autistic, or LGBTQ+. As if that's not enough, women often have to overcome the internal pressure that they put on themselves.

It's hard to quantify, but it's the kind of thing most people have seen. Men can walk into any conversation way more confidently than women in the exact same position. It's not fair and I wish it wasn't the case, but at the end of the day, it comes down to what you can control and what you can't control. You can't control people's perception of you – at least not in the beginning. You can't control their biases or their expectations. You may not even be able to control how you feel, but you can control how prepared you are, you can control how you show up, and you can control how clearly you communicate. The way to do that is through meticulous preparation.

IMPACTFUL COMMUNICATION

One powerful way to build your confidence and move past impostor syndrome is to focus on impactful communication. What I've found is that the higher up the ladder you go, the more important your speaking style becomes. Executives don't have a lot of time, so as you climb the corporate ladder and interact with executives, know that brevity is your friend. That means getting to the punchline faster.

Even when you communicate with them over an email, they'll most likely be reading it on a phone, so you must make sure that the most important points are prominent and concise. Action items, recommendations, and suggestions should stand out first. Then, if they need more details, they can dig into the rest of your message.

The hallmark of executive communication is to be direct and convey the most important information or action you need from them right up front rather than taking your readers through an entire story. Brevity, being concise, and having clear suggestions will earn you respect as a clear communicator and someone that has thought deeply about the content ahead of time.

NEGOTIATE FOR WHAT YOU WANT AND DESERVE

When I was a junior buyer in the purchasing department at ADIC, my first job out of college, I developed a reputation for being a bulldog negotiator. The company was growing by triple-digits year over year. We were manufacturing tape storage computer hardware products in-house at the time. This was twenty plus years ago when companies were still using backup tapes to back up all the critical data, way before cloud storage. To assemble a tape storage library product, literally took hundreds if not thousands of parts, which all were sourced by the purchasing department. One of the components I was responsible for procuring and to ensure we never ran out was tape media. They were like cassette tapes for the recording of back up data. Tape media was a commodity component and there were three vendors we regularly used for our supply. We were not only tasked with getting all required components, in the right amount, we had to do it at the best possible price.

Having played team sports since junior high, I'm very competitive and I always strive for my team to win. Naturally it was my nature to keep pushing my vendors for a better deal. I was fresh out of college and hadn't learned where the line was between pushing hard for the best deal and pushing so hard that I'd hurt the relationship.

One day my manager, Peter, pulled me aside and said, "Let's just go with what we've got on the tape media." I said, "Wait, I think I can get the price down even further." Obviously, I didn't get the message Peter was trying to send.

He proceeded to share with me that to build a long lasting and successful partnership with our vendors, we needed to find a "win-win" solution for both parties. The worst thing that could happen is that we push too hard, the vendors stop making money, and eventually have to exit the business. He also shared that if we build a strong relationship with them, they're more likely to work with us when the supply gets tight.

It was his subtle way of telling me that pushing too hard could sour the relationship. The takeaway for me was that no matter who you negotiate with, you want to come out where both sides feel like they've won. From then on, I kept in mind that if I win and the other party loses, it's also a loss for me because it hurts the relationship.

I've learned that it's WAY easier for me to negotiate a business deal than a personal one. In a business deal, it's very fact-based and there is very little emotion attached. But to negotiate for something I really want, all my logic gets thrown out the window. That's also why I've never walked into a car dealership alone. I always bring my "lead negotiator" with me. In the early days, that would be my mom, and later, my husband.

Negotiating for a car is still a lot less stressful than negotiating for a job. And I'm here to tell you that it was hard for me too. When you've gone through a rigorous interview process and decided to say yes to a job, all you want to do is to get started. You are not alone.

But don't let that stop you from negotiating for what you deserve.

According to a 2016 Glassdoor Salary Negotiation Insights Survey, nearly three in five U.S. employees accepted the first package they were offered with no negotiation. More alarming, 68% of female respondents did not negotiate salary vs. 52% of the male respondents.

A corporate recruiter had told me that female applicants were often hesitant to push back, fearing they would be seen as greedy. But it's important to be your own advocate, and equally important to be confident and well informed when negotiating.

Like others, I find the negotiation process uncomfortable. At the same time, it's important to not have "buyer's remorse" with "woulda, shoulda, coulda" thoughts. For me, it always comes down to the facts. The facts have always helped me determine what's great, what's good, and when to walk away.

1). Do Your Homework

One of the great frameworks I learned from the Negotiation class during my Executive MBA program at Cornell is that before you enter a negotiation, you should have already identified your ideal outcome, your minimum acceptable outcome, and somewhere in between is likely where the agreement will be.

Before even considering a number, visit sites like Payscale and Glassdoor which provide you salary averages based on your experience level and location. Speaking of location, if you are moving to a new state or country, be sure to research the cost of living. The same salary in Arkansas and New York City translates into a very different lifestyle.

Another mistake a candidate can make in the negotiating process is to only focus on the base salary. In the US, state by state taxation laws should be as important as any other factor in accepting a role. The same applies if you're considering a role in other countries. Here are some factors to consider:

- If relocation is involved domestically in the US, is there a state income tax, and how much? What are the different brackets?

- If relocation is involved internationally, how will you be taxed and whether your company will give you tax preparation assistance?
- How are bonuses paid and taxed?
- How does the cost of living, rental, and property tax compared to their current situation?
- Can I keep the rest of my relocation package/bonus if I don't use it all in the move?

2). Your Salary is Just the Beginning

While negotiating your salary is important, don't lose sight of the total compensation package. Depending on industry or specific companies, signing bonuses, performance-based awards, stock options and company equity are all important factors to supplementing your income. Healthcare benefits vary significantly from company to company. Over-time earnings, retirement matching programs and payment for unused vacation days are also something to remember.

3). Think Beyond the Paycheck

Office culture, work-life balance, and opportunities for growth are equally important as the number in your paycheck. If you need to work from home on a particular day, or if you need to be at your child's game every Friday - mention that up front.

One of the "Future of Work" trends that got accelerated during the COVID-19 Pandemic is flexibility in work schedule. While some companies were starting to offer work-at-home before the pandemic, working from home became the only way to work for most non-essential workers when governments across the world went into lockdown mode. Many employers are more open than ever to offering employees work-from-home days if desired. If this is important to you, be sure to ask for what you need up front.

4). Seek Opportunities for Growth

To me, an important perk is executive coaching. This is a win-win for you and your new employer as it provides the opportunity for personal growth and professional success. Tuition reimbursement, leadership programs and access to industry events, networking summits are also ways to help you stay current with your industry or function.

After a long job search, it's more than understandable that you just want to accept and get started, but it is important you do your homework to start with the right foot to maintain your work-life integration and accelerate your career on the table. Your prospective employer wants you to begin a new chapter in your career journey with 100% commitment and motivation so that all parties can be successful.

Key Takeaways

- **Build Your Leadership Voice**: Figure out who you are as a leader. You don't have to have a title to be a leader. Instead, focus on being the best you can be at your job and identify how your skills can position you for the next step in your career.
- **Tune Out the Noise**: We all lack confidence at one point or another. We feel self-conscious and start listening to the voices, whether external or internal, that tell us we aren't good enough. Practice, planning, and preparation are the best ways to overcome "impostor syndrome".
- **Negotiate for What You Deserve**: Negotiate for what you deserve, even if it means having to walk away from an opportunity. At the same time, look

at the total compensation package, not just the salary figure when you're evaluating a role.

———

5

MOVING UP THE LADDER

As you continue to grow your career, keep in mind that the only way you can be successful is to bring people along with you. In other words, you have to become a leader that people want to follow - even if you aren't in a leadership role. This is true whether you work in a startup or a large multinational corporation.

Wherever you are, it's about knowing what drives people, teams, and ultimately, organizations. What vision can you connect with? How can you align your goals with your teams' goals? How can you lead and inspire them so that your team wants to follow your lead? And how can you build a recognizable leadership brand that gets the attention of your leaders and sponsors?

I already shared the story of Dan, where I went from "How do I become more like Dan as a people manager?" to realizing "No, I don't want to become like Dan, because that means that I'm not being authentic to myself. This isn't a popularity contest. This is about me being comfortable with and owning who I am and attracting people who will see the vision of where I want to go."

When I went to SAP, there were people who had been on my team at Microsoft and Level 3 who decided to follow me into the new company because of the vision of how I wanted to build the organization, the overall culture, and the focus of the company. It was such a privilege to have people follow me and benefit my new employer with their talent. I took the careers of the leaders on my team very seriously and asked myself "What does this role mean to people individually? What does it mean to their own personal growth?" Yes, I built a reputation for being direct and challenging my team, but they also knew that I wanted the best for them and cared about their personal and professional happiness. To me, that's how you can build belonging.

The same applies to my friend Brian Reaves, who recently left his role as the Chief Diversity and Inclusion Officer at Dell Technologies for the inaugural role of Chief Belonging, Diversity, and Equity Officer at UKG. I first met Brian when he was a colleague of mine at SAP heading up Diversity and Inclusion for the CEO Board Area. Brian is a high energy guy with such warmth. Not only is he passionate about diversity and technologies, what I remember most about Brian is that he always helped give other leaders, especially Black leaders, visibility to other senior leaders. On numerous occasions when I bumped into Brian, he would introduce me to high potential leaders in the company. When he went to Dell, I wasn't surprised that people followed him because of his brand and reputation as a leader.

A question I often get especially in Town Hall meetings with early talents, a term SAP uses to describe employees who are recent graduates, "Maggie, I'm just starting out in my career. I have limited work experience. How do I grow?"

It's an excellent question and my response to anyone earlier in their career is to become really good at what they do. At that level, being a talent magnet means that you're so good at what you do that others want to learn from you. People want you to be on their team or to help them with their projects. When people come to you for advice and ask you to share your best practices, you know that you're poised for growth.

Sometimes people feel like sharing their best practices is a form of bragging. As a leader, I look at it completely differently. Sharing best practices, when done with the intention to help others in the organization, lifts your entire team, and even the broader organization performs better. It cements your reputation as a team player, and a leader. When you help the team perform better collectively, you naturally draw attention to yourself as high-performance talent with leadership potential. When you shift to saying, "I'm not doing this in a way that is bragging, I'm doing it in a way that can benefit other parts of the organization so that we can move faster toward our goals", it's a team win. How? Don't just share the win, share how you got there. What were the lessons and insights you learned along the way that others can learn from to either accelerate the business or avoid the mistakes you had made.

MANAGING UP, DOWN, AND ACROSS

Even early in your career, you have the potential to manage up and across, starting with your very first job. Sometimes, managing up gets a bad rap, as if you're a teacher's pet, but it simply means that you're aligning your goals with the goals of your superiors'.

An organization performs at its best when the goals and the execution are completely aligned across the entire organization. Managing up means understanding how you align your objectives with your superiors, with your managers, your manager's managers, and the broader organization. It comes down to communicating with your leaders so that they know that you're working toward department goals.

Recently, I received a LinkedIn message from someone who heard me sharing advice about this goal-alignment topic two years prior. She said, "To this day I remember the advice you gave on the panel discussion: 'Make sure your work is tightly aligned with your boss' targets and goals' I followed your advice and my career benefited from making that shift!" Getting that message totally made my day.

Managing across is about managing your relationship with your peers. Peers share a common bond of being in the trenches along with you. Whether you're working on similar areas in a group, or across different groups, the key question is, how do you share best practices with your peers? Most are pretty good at managing up, but managing across, and aligning your goals with your peers' goals requires more focus. Sometimes you understand how your goals align with your manager's goals, but you may not know how to align your goals with your peers' goals. So even just understanding where your peers are coming from, and how you can help support one another, is quite helpful.

As you continue to climb the ladder, you'll have to manage down, up, and across. Most people do their best in managing down because they feel like it's their team. But I remind people that your very first team is your peer group. This is the team that you as a team member are working with to contribute to the broader organization's success, so learning how to collaborate with them is key.

One of the things that I really appreciated about Dan as my manager back in my Microsoft days was that he was good at making people feel welcome. When I first joined his group, he helped me figure out how I fit into the culture of the group. Microsoft's cloud business was in the early days of explosive growth and becoming more and more critical to the overall growth of the organization. When I was promoted to a director and reported directly to Fred, the General Manager, Dan became a peer of mine. It could have been awkward, but because we had such a great relationship, a relationship that we both invested in, when I became his peer, we continued to have a strong relationship. Dan was proud to see me in my new role, making our relationship even stronger over time.

If you're good at what you do, it's not uncommon for you to end up getting promoted and even managing former peers. Even earlier in my career, when I was still in my twenties, I became a leader in a group at Sun Microsystems for the first time. I was leading a small team of three people who used to be my peers, and at the beginning, it was a bit awkward. We started as peers, and I ended up being their manager.

To manage the tension, I wiped the slate clean and started speaking with my team members individually about their career aspirations, their motivation and how I can best support them. If you find yourself in the same situation, the good news is that you already know the people on your team. You may know what they're working on and what they're good at.

This is a golden opportunity to discover what motivates them. What do they want to grow into? How can you help them grow their career? How can you help them remove roadblocks on their projects? Just like you want to align your goals with your manager's goals, you build this new relationship with your former peers by learning their goals, their motivation triggers, and helping them achieve them. Suddenly you go from being a potential threat to an ally in a position to help them achieve their goals.

There will be times where your former peers may have expected themselves to get your role. Or your promotion may trigger them to leave the team or the company, and it happens. They'll likely look for other opportunities elsewhere inside or outside the company. In fact, you'll want to identify the team members who are committed to the direction you're heading and those who aren't quickly, so you can build a high-performance team.

LEADING WITHOUT AUTHORITY

One of the things that I hear people say when they are trying to become a first-time manager is, "I'm not a leader because I don't manage people." I remind them that they don't have to directly manage people to be a leader. A leader is someone that other people want to follow. A kindergartener helping another frightened kindergartener on his first day of school is a leader. Leadership isn't a title, it's an action – and anyone can do it.

One experienced manager I know advises people who wanted to be first time managers to find three people who would say, "Yes, I would love to join your team when you build a team one day", because that showed that the prospective manager was ready to lead. Leading before you have authority is a precursor to becoming a great people manager.

Perfecting your craft is the most important thing you can do to be viewed as a leader - especially early on in your career.

People naturally view you as a domain expert – that includes your peers as well as your managers. If you work in a large organization, you'll most likely work closely with other teams on projects and can easily build a reputation outside of your own team if you're on top of your game. Conveying your expertise positions you as high-performing talent with leadership potential. Mastering your craft identifies you as a leader and attracts the attention not only of your direct superiors, but from other leaders within the organization.

Most of us have a direct chain of command and assume that it's sufficient to achieve the immediate goals of our manager and team. The reality is organizations are like a symphony with many instruments that need to play in harmony with each other. Cross-group collaboration continues to be a critical skill as you move up the ladder. Like a beautiful piece of music played by a symphony, companies perform at their peak when they can align their departments to achieve an overall goal.

FEEDBACK IS A GIFT

"Women are not always provided honest feedback because of the perception that they will not receive it well." That's a controversial statement for sure, but it's what a very successful female executive once shared with me. I can't help but wonder how many other managers, male and female alike, feel that same way toward their female team members.

In contrast, a high-powered telecom executive once shared with me "in my eyes, feedback is a gift that always holds a nugget of truth, positive or negative. You can only receive this gift if you are humble enough to accept it and apply it in a constructive way." She went on to say "When my career was slowing, I asked my peers for honest feedback. After much praise, one peer provided me with the feedback I needed to grow. He said I was mothering my team rather than leading. He went on to say that because I wanted everyone to do well, I sometimes shouldered everyone's responsibilities vs. holding them accountable. I quickly adapted my leadership style to hold my entire team accountable. It was then that I understood the gift of feedback and how important honest, consistent communication is to one's success."

That story illustrates not only the power of feedback, but that feedback is only helpful if it comes from people that you respect and trust. Sometimes we ask people for feedback, but if you don't trust the person that you're asking, then you probably won't use, or even listen to the feedback. When you get feedback from people you trust, you know the feedback is coming from the right place. Even if it's harsh, you'll still be inclined to look inward and ask, "How can I use this in a way to help myself to be better".

Give yourself room to take the feedback in and digest it, internalize it, and think about how you can learn from it. Also give yourself room to decode what feedback is truly helpful and what feedback you can disregard. Feedback can often trigger emotions of fear, judgement, embarrassment, or inadequacy, so it's important to give yourself time to process it - especially if it's hard to swallow at first.

When I decided to become an entrepreneur, I went to a startup boot camp. For thirteen weeks, I was with a group of entrepreneurs who were building their dreams. One of the things we were asked to do was to get advice from trusted advisors or mentors who have experience building their own startups. I often heard other entrepreneurs blame negative outcomes on "bad advice" from a mentor or advisor.

My take is that you have to own your own actions. Advice is just advice. It's merely a point of view. You can take that advice as input - but how you process that input and turn it into action is up to you. I recommend that people take each piece of feedback as such, and then process it from their own angle so they can apply it to their own context. By separating the wheat from the chaff and sorting out good advice from bad advice, you assume full responsibility, and control, of your outcomes.

As with anything new, you're bound to make mistakes and bad decisions. I call these mistakes "tuitions". Sometimes you will just have to "pay" for the mistakes and hopefully learn the lesson and gain some new insights.

SHARED GOALS

I'm always honored when past colleagues, or even bosses, ask me to have a mentoring discussion with their daughters. I always say yes because of the impact they have made on my career and what a great way for me to say "thank you" and pay it forward to the next generation leaders.

It's one of these scenarios that I met a high-energy woman who started a new job at Microsoft during the COVID-19 pandemic. Her mom connected us and hoped I could share some tips with her daughter on how best to navigate such a massive and matrixed organization that I've been speaking highly of from my own experience, not to mention the added virtual working experience. Because she joined the team during the height of the pandemic, she had never met any of her team members or managers in person - everything was done through Microsoft Teams, a video conferencing and collaboration software application. After speaking to her, I could tell that she is very talented and driven, and eager to make an impact in her new role.

She shared with me that she had previously worked in much smaller companies and the biggest team she'd been part of was 30 people, at most. Now she'd taken a job at a company with over 100,000 employees.

Because of my Microsoft experience, she asked me, "How do I navigate in this environment? I feel like I'm talking to a lot of teams, but how do I move things forward?" I asked, "Have you had one-on-one conversations with people that you collaborate with in different parts of your organization? Have you asked them what their goals and objectives are?"

I explained that her goal may be to launch this product whereas she may be working with a team whose goal is to increase the number of partners in their ecosystem. The question is "How do you connect the dots between the two so that you can find that win-win scenario?" I also explained that goals in large companies change or adjust every year, sometimes more often, so it's important to revisit that conversation because it will strengthen the relationship and make sure that you're both helping each other achieve the right goal at the right time.

That was a lightbulb moment for her, because when she was working in a much smaller company, everyone shared the same goals and knew what everyone else was working on. Since she never had experience working for such a big company, it never occurred to her to find out what people in different departments were trying to accomplish. She had not even considered that they may have different business objectives. Once she realized that, she was able to ask the right questions so she could align what she was doing with their goals and create a win-win scenario. Then it's a matter of communicating that you understand their goals and are focused on helping them achieve them.

While you're thinking about your own career roadmap and chasing your North Star, you have to excel in the "here and now" of where you are. Being a team player and knowing everyone's "position" will help mobilize the team to reach the broader team goals and get you noticed, fast.

I had to learn to do the same thing at Microsoft when launching our cloud product in the US market. I was new into my role and started working with a guy who was the head of sales for the US market. There was a lot of tension between us, to say the least. He had an aggressive, "in your face" type of communication style. It was the very early days of cloud computing, and the first year for our Software-as-a-Service (SaaS) products. We were struggling in the market and weren't hitting our targets. In fact, we were only hitting a fraction of our goals. Since the category was so new, we didn't even know if our goals were realistic.

That said, I was committed to helping him and his team be successful, so I asked him a lot of questions. I was trying to understand the business landscape, the types of objections he was hearing from customers, insights from our sellers and partners, so I could get a sense of what wasn't working. I was hoping to identify those friction points so we could improve our marketing and handle those objections via our marketing efforts so that it would be easier for him to sell.

As it turned out, he didn't think I was being helpful, and instead viewed my questions as if I was questioning him. What I didn't know at that time was that the team was under a lot of scrutiny because it was such an important product category for the company. He was probably feeling the fatigue of the constant questioning of the health of the business.

As a result, things got tense between us very fast (as if things weren't bad enough already). In fact, it was so bad that I had to go to my skip-level manager Fred and tell him "I can't work with this guy. His tone and language is just too aggressive and disrespectful". Fred spoke with this sales leader and let him know that his approach was making me feel uncomfortable. It was awkward, but it had to be done.

To his credit, the sales leader came to me and apologized and said, "You know Maggie, I'd love to hit the 'restart' button and discuss how we can help each other".

When he did that, I was able to tell him that the only reason I was asking him so many questions was to understand the landscape that he was dealing with and the objections he was facing from his customers so I could help him hit his sales goals.

I reassured him "I'm here to help. We have a shared goal. If you hit your sales goals, that means I'm hitting my goals, so I want to do what I can to make you successful".

In that process, we learned that our market didn't even understand the point of moving to "the cloud". Since the concept was so new, it was very hard to sell – even to our existing customers. In terms of targeting, we made some assumptions early on, assuming that mid-market enterprise companies would be our sweet spot as early adopters. As we continued our journey, we realized that our early hypothesis was wrong. We did some quantitative and quali-tative research and discovered that our earliest adopters were, paradoxically, small and medium businesses (SMB) and large enterprises.

SMBs loved the idea of using the same productivity tools as big enterprises and didn't want to incur the upfront licensing costs of traditional software. Large enterprises saw the competitive advantage of moving to the cloud and freeing up their valuable internal technical resources on strategic initiatives. Once we figured out our sweet spot target audiences, and how our product could add value to them, we were off to the races. But we couldn't have done it if the sales leader and I hadn't been able to set our differences aside and get to the root of the problem together.

That interaction cemented our relationship and laid the foundation for tight collaboration and success between our two teams. From that point forward, we hit our goals every single quarter. We played off of the healthy tension that's inherent between most marketing and sales teams so we could set each other up for success. Understanding where we were each coming from and aligning our goals and key performance indicators (KPIs) to each other was what made our relationship work so well - despite having started too poorly.

Creating shared goals; with your team, with your manager, and with other teams is the hallmark of a great collaborator.

DEALING WITH SETBACKS

Everyone's leadership journey is marked with setbacks; they just aren't usually in the public eye.

There's a famous piece of advice that says, "Don't compare your 'behind the scenes' with someone else's highlight reel". It's easy to read about someone's accolades and accomplishments and feel inadequate. But I'll tell you from firsthand experience that things are never what they seem, and that the fastest way to feel like a failure is to compare yourself to others.

Rest assured that even the most "successful" people fall - and when they do - they fall *hard*. Just like every leader can spout off his or her list of accomplishments, they usually have their fair share of battle scars and disaster stories to share.

One of the setbacks in my career happened when I was at Microsoft. You may recall that I had been offered a position to lead a business unit marketing team in China, which was an absolute thrill. You may also recall that I eventually turned that opportunity down and went to Level 3 Communications. But there are some details behind the story that make it more, let's just say, colorful.

Before any of that transpired, I was informed by my manager about an upcoming position at Microsoft to lead the U.S. public sector marketing team. Now this was at the tail end of the Microsoft Office 365 cloud launch, which went incredibly well. We were getting market traction, and my team and I got recognition within Microsoft for the successful launch.

Riding the wave of that success, I felt invincible. I felt like I had accomplished what I had set out to do in this role. It became apparent to me that it was time to think about the next challenge I wanted to take on.

I was very much thinking of staying at Microsoft. Afterall, I loved the company, I loved everything the company was doing, I loved my team, and I loved my managers. It was a great position that allowed me the ability to express myself and realize my full potential.

At that time my manager, Angus, and I had been having career development conversations already. While an international assignment was still in the back of my mind, there wasn't any role open that would be a fit for me at that time. Angus knew that I wanted to grow and was looking for a new role and he wanted to support me to find it. As the cloud business was rapidly growing, it was time to merge the Microsoft Office 365 cloud team with the Microsoft Office traditional software team into one department and asked if I wanted to lead it.

Combined, it would be a larger team with more responsibility and a bigger challenge. This role would also offer me an opportunity to become a manager of managers. But deep down, I felt that the role wasn't different enough. I've always considered myself a lifelong learner. I'm excited by new roles because I get to learn new things. I wanted something completely new that I could apply my creativity and my ingenuity to. So I politely declined and decided to look for a position outside of that department.

At the end of the day, I wanted to learn something new, increase my skills and get exposure to other parts of the business; all of which was part of my career roadmap. It was very important for me to build more competencies. And that's what made the decision so much easier for me.

Angus, always looking out for me, caught wind of a role to head up marketing over the public sector business, meaning all of Microsoft's business with federal, state, and local governments in the US, and was kind enough to tell me about it.

It was a very interesting role because the public sector was a market segment I had not had direct experience yet, and it would also be a manager of managers role.

It made so much sense because I had helped bring Microsoft's cloud business to the private sector. The public sector was starting to warm up to the idea of cloud computing, I figured I could take my learnings and apply them there. Best of all, Angus told me that with an upcoming reorg, the role will report directly to his manager, Allison.

That meant if I got that job, we would both report to his boss who was already a sponsor of mine, making me his peer. It was an awesome opportunity, and I was incredibly excited about it, so I decided to take a shot at it and threw my hat in the ring.

As I went through the interviews, I felt confident. Afterall, I had a good track record, was viewed as a high-potential employee, and had the support of my boss, the hiring manager, and her boss, who happened to be the president of the North America region.

My excitement hit a brick wall when the head of the public sector interviewed me. I'll spare you the details, but the organizational restructure was changing, and that role was going to report into marketing (as opposed to the head of the public sector), so that leader wanted to ensure the person selected in the role was someone he could trust.

I also know what I wouldn't bring to the table – my weakness for the role - direct public sector experience. The other candidate interviewing for this role was already on the Public Sector Marketing team. Suffice it to say, in his eyes, the other candidate was a safer bet, already knowing the sector and having a great working relationship with him.

But I'm always up for a challenge, so I read all the strategy papers, spoke with people I knew in that business, and prepared myself to take the role. While I lacked public sector experience, my cloud experience was crucial in where this business is heading. I went through the interview process and felt confident that I would get the job.

After the interview process, I didn't hear back for several weeks. During that time, my confidence started to dissipate, but I still had hope because I knew that the public sector was ripe for Microsoft's cloud services. Time went on, and I still hadn't heard back about that position. This is the same time that I started having conversations about that international assignment in China. I shared with Allison that if I were to get the public sector job, I would not continue to interview for other roles. I was hoping that every small step could help me land that job.

It wasn't just me who was confident about the job, Angus, my manager, had already privately shared with some of my peers that I would get that job.

It was springtime, which in Microsoft's rhythm of business, was the time that the top executives from across the world gather at the Microsoft Conference Center in Redmond, Washington to discuss the upcoming fiscal year. That year, I was fortunate enough to be invited to this event as a high potential leader, hearing directly from the very top executives of the company on our goals and steps to achieve them.

At some point during the day, Allison saw me and said, "Hey, Maggie, can I talk to you?" I remember sitting on one of the benches outside of the conference when she told me, "I want to personally tell you, unfortunately, you did not get that head of marketing public sector job."

"What?? How could it be?" I thought to myself. At that moment, I felt like a complete failure. With all the interview preparations, and the results the team was able to accomplish on the cloud business, there was nothing more I could do to change the outcome. I should also mention that during this process, my beloved grandmother passed away in Hong Kong. I hadn't had the opportunity to properly grieve yet. The news hit me like a ton of bricks.

To make things worse, my manager, Angus, had already offered the job to head up the combined Microsoft

Office/365 team to someone else. He knew I wasn't interested in it, and since he was so confident that I'd get that public sector role, he already gave that job to my peer running the Microsoft Office marketing team.

This made Allison's news sting so much more. I essentially was in limbo; I didn't get the job that I wanted, and I couldn't fall back on the job that I thought I still had.

I was overwhelmed with emotion. I remember tears streaming down my face while I was still struggling to have this conversation with Allison. I asked why I didn't get the job and was told that the head of the public sector division wanted someone with public sector experience.

She went on to ask if I had any questions, and I remember making up some questions to be polite, but I didn't want to talk about it anymore. I felt so down and disappointed that I just wanted to leave and head home.

Despite the high-level sponsorships from my management chain of command, my proven track record, and my designation as a high-performance employee, I still didn't get the job – and it all boiled down to not having experience in the public sector. It was just too much for me to process. I felt that I never had a chance to land that job because, in my view, the public sector leader had already made up his mind before the interview process began.

So I just cried and didn't try to hold it back. There has always been a stigma for a woman to cry or show emotions at work. When people ask me if it's ok to cry at work, I say that, done sparingly, it's very powerful to show your emotions because it illustrates how much you truly care. Over the years, I have built a tough exterior, so seeing me cry showed just how let down I was.

It wasn't until I was a senior executive that I understood the tough position Allison was in. I've had marketing leaders who I thought would be great for field marketing positions. However, I learned that if the sales leader doesn't share that view, it just won't work. In hindsight, I see why I didn't get that public sector job – it wasn't that I was inadequate, I just wasn't the right fit for what they were looking for.

As painful as that experience was, and as disappointed as I was, it led to many good things. I believe that when one door closes, another (or a few others) opens. Because I didn't get the public sector job, my management and sponsors went into retention mode – they clearly didn't want me to leave the company and were quick to help find a role for me within the company.

I was even given a rare one-on-one discussion with then the President of the North America region, reiterating how much they valued me as a talent and how they'd work to help me land my next role. Soon after, I was asked to interview for multiple positions, and was eventually offered a few roles to choose from, including an international assignment to go to Beijing, China that I mentioned in a previous chapter. The interview process gave me so much exposure within the company and I got a lot of one-on-one time with leaders of other departments that I never would have had if I were to be offered that public sector position.

Given all the uncertainties about my future, I also interviewed for and received an offer for an external senior executive role at Level 3 Communications. Looking back, not getting that public sector ended up being exactly what I needed to hit my North Star goal of being the CMO.

Setbacks happen, but like Winston Churchill's famous quote goes, "Success is not final, failure is not fatal: It is the courage to continue that counts."

THE ROLE OF LUCK

In 2018, I was giving a leadership lecture at Cornell Johnson business school. During the Q&A section, one of the male students raised his hand and asked "Maggie, given your career success, do you think that luck has played a role in your success?" I responded by saying "Yes" and went on to explain how luck factored into my success.

After the presentation, the professor that invited me to speak, who was a woman, said to me, "You know Maggie, I really didn't like that question." She explained that if I were a man, she didn't think I would get that question. I nodded and told her that I wasn't offended by it. In fact, I thought it led to a great discussion about luck and the role that luck plays in success. It also did make me curious about whether successful males talk about the effect of luck in their success.

Through that process, I've come to believe that luck plays a role in everyone's success, regardless of gender, race, or culture. But I also believe that we have a role in creating our luck. To me, luck is simply when opportunity meets preparation.

Everyone has the power to prepare. That's when you plant the seeds of opportunity to sprout for them in the future. Any time a leader asks me for advice when they are looking for a new role, I ask them to crystalize what they are looking for such as type of role, size of company, industry, location; then mobilize their network by letting people know you're in the market for a new role.

It is not uncommon that when you see someone updating their LinkedIn profiles, you may think that they are in the market for a new job. It's because that's where most recruiters find candidates. That's an intentional decision that will help attract "luck".

I remember while at Level 3, CEO Jeff Storey had shared a quote which became one of my favorites. He said, "Chance favors the prepared mind", by the French scientist Louis Pasteur. Jeff was sharing the quote on how we needed to be at our best to service our customers and capture market opportunities.

The quote also applies to how we manage our own career. When you're preparing yourself for your next role, you need to acquire the skills, expertise, and connections that would help get you there. That way, when the opportunity presents itself, you're ready. The worst thing that can happen is when an opportunity presents itself, you aren't ready for it. You have to prepare, sharpen your skills, grow your network, cultivate relationships, and constantly help others before you ever call in favors or expect "luck" to magically be on your side.

On the flip side, it can feel extremely frustrating when you feel like you're down on luck. The good news is that there are things you can do when luck and opportunity do not present themselves. In fact, I once worked with a mentee who was in the exact same scenario. She was an executive at a Fortune 500 technology company when I first met her and was doing extremely well in her role. She was eventually poached by an even larger technology company to take on a bigger role, and I was super excited for her. She's smart, hardworking, and has a great work ethic.

I later found out that she left that company two years into her tenure there. She was going through a lot of personal challenges at the same time, which made it hard for her to balance a highly demanding job and personal life. Eventually, she decided to take some time off and focus on her personal life. I supported her decision and was happy to hear that she's taking time to recalibrate.

When she returned to the workforce, she got an executive role at a new company, but sadly, she didn't end up staying there for very long. Knowing her situation, and that I was part of her support system, I decided to reach out and check in on her.

She was very appreciative of my outreach and my advice to focus on the things that she could control, which are her own actions. I empathized with her and reassured her that plenty of great people have hard times in their career. It didn't mean that she was deficient, and it wasn't a strike against her in any way. I reminded her that sometimes opportunities just don't pan out. All you can do in that situation is keep pushing forward, keep networking, and keep preparing yourself for that next opportunity. If you continue to lay the groundwork and keep planting seeds, opportunity will eventually present itself. Things may look bleak in the moment, but they end up working out in the end – just like what happened with that public sector job I thought I was going to get.

In his now famous 2005 Stanford commencement speech, Steve Jobs shared some insightful advice. A story I remember most is when he talked about dropping in on a calligraphy class after dropping out of Reed College. What he learned in that class which seemed to have no practical use at the time became distinctive features in Apple's very first Macintosh computer 10 years later. The moral of the story is that you can never connect the dots looking forward, you can only connect the dots looking backwards. For me, I trust that everything happens for a reason, there's meaning to everything you experience if you can capture the "essence" of it.

There will be hardships along the way. They might hurt, and they may not make sense at the moment, but it's important to pick yourself up, dust yourself off, and keep moving forward. One day, when you look back, everything will end up being worthwhile because of the lessons you'll have learned, no matter how stinging pain is in the moment.

BUILDING NEW MUSCLES

Speaking of pain, when I got to Level 3, I questioned whether I even made the right decision. I had a similar "buyer's remorse" when I first went from Sun to Microsoft too, but for an entirely different reason. Despite it being a great opportunity for me, it came with an entirely new set of challenges. As part of the business transformation and its quest for profitability, the company was going through a major restructuring to capture synergy from the acquisition of Global Crossing. It was a major transformation rife with layoffs.

As a leader, I believe that having to let good talent go is the hardest thing to do. In my first few quarters, I was forced to look at my org chart and decide which positions I could cut. Up until this point, I had never experienced such a massive turnaround situation. Not only did it weigh heavily on me personally, but I also felt like I was inadequate to handle the situation.

That's where my support system came into play. One of my good friends Jackie, whom I had met during my early days at Microsoft, is an astute finance leader. She shared with me how one of the major retailers she had worked for navigated a major turnaround by protecting what was truly the core to the business. That was helpful and gave me perspective; I did have to cut jobs, but it was in order to save other jobs and position the company as a whole for growth.

During that time, I also spoke with my coach Mary for guidance. Having Mary as my "safe space" was so critical, which is why I tell every leader to get a coach. Being completely vulnerable, I said to Mary, "I cannot do this. I don't know how to let more people go, while also keeping all the balls in the air and not let any projects drop." Mary, always in her calm and caring voice, first acknowledged my angst, then said "What if you think about this as building new muscles. It's true that you may not have gone through such a turnaround, but you have mastered many business challenges. What do you think you need to do to turn this around?"

That was it, another one of my lightbulb moments, this experience is about building new muscles. And I took Jackie's advice to "protect the core" and identified projects to cut out completely instead of trying to do everything with insufficient resources.

It was challenging, but some of my fondest memories at Level 3 was not only learning from the shrewd executive leadership team in leading the company to profitability for the first time, but the fact that I worked at a company that truly valued diversity, inclusion and belonging. With the backdrop of the Rocky Mountains in Colorado, where Level 3 was headquartered, I also felt people walked the talk about work life balance. I rarely got work emails on the weekend unless we were in the midst of a critical situation.

In hindsight, when I looked back and connected the dots, I needed to add the new muscles and I could not ask for a more inclusive team and environment to help me step into senior executive management.

And now, any time when I have executives come saying they have "buyer's remorse" in jumping to a new company, I say "Give it a year". For the most part, when you head to a new company, especially after a long tenure in the former company, it is a shock to the system. You have to learn and adjust to the new culture, and ways to get things done. And you have to rebuild your credibility that you most likely took for granted in your old role. Most of these executives ended up feeling more comfortable after a year and many go on and thrive in the new company.

The learning for me there was to lean into the discomfort and remember that there's a reason for each chapter of your career journey. It may not be clear or maybe it's even confusing when you were in the middle of it, but when you look back, it'll all make sense.

HOW DO I PIVOT?

So you've activated your leadership journey. You're following your roadmap to your career North Star and things are going great. Until they don't and you're forced to pivot. Or, what if, after some time, what you're doing no longer excites you, and you change your mind?

Maybe you're exposed to another area and discover a passion for something else. Maybe you accomplish your goal and decide you want to take on something new. Or you discover that your industry is taking stances that aren't congruent with your values. Maybe you're forced to pivot because the company is struggling.

Regardless of the reason, pivoting is something that all of us will likely face at one point or another. It may be inevitable, but if you can be intentional about it, you can soften the impact.

For example, my pivot from a corporate executive to an entrepreneur wasn't on my career roadmap, but the passion that I had for helping next-generation leaders grow, especially those in underrepresented groups, drove me to pivot into launching my own business.

Earlier in my career I focused almost exclusively on my professional growth. As I rose through the ranks in corporate America, I focused on gaining financial independence. Once I accomplished those areas of focus, I pivoted toward my personal values. Entrepreneurship was a vehicle to help me focus on my passion for advancing equity leadership for women and other minorities. I wanted to inject my leadership voice into creating a more equitable workplace.

A part of me still loves tackling big transformational challenges in the corporate environment, so a career as a board director made perfect sense in the next chapter of what many called a "portfolio career", a career that encompasses several related or unrelated jobs.

It's quite common for professionals to want to pivot from one industry to another. AJ, one of the people I mentored, was introduced to me by one of Tenshey's coaches. AJ was accepted to the Cornell executive MBA program; the same one I did a decade prior. AJ once said to me "Maggie, I'm in the healthcare industry and really want to pivot into tech. How do I do that?" My advice is to take stock of their transferable skills. When you think of cross team collaboration, leadership, analytical skills, or creative skills - they lend themselves to any number of fields. Whether you're in healthcare and want to pivot into tech, or whether you're in finance and want to pivot into marketing, take stock of what you do well and how you can add value in a different domain.

In AJ's case, her transferable skills from her experience in a large healthcare company included customer account management, project management, and strong analytical and cross-group collaboration skills.

Too often we assume we aren't qualified because we haven't "done it". Many recruiters may look for candidates who have "been there and done that" because those are safer choices, but you only need one company to say "yes". Your job is to position yourself and convey how your unique blend of skills and experiences can help your new organization. Doing so instantly makes you a strong candidate, despite being an industry outsider.

Going back to AJ's story, when she got an interview with a major tech company, she went all in on the prep. She spent a lot of time understanding the company's vision, strategic direction, and how she could add value. She spent time with her executive coach to ensure her own limiting beliefs didn't jeopardize her chance of getting her dream job.

I suggested that she identify potential questions from the interviewers and run through a mock interview with a friend. She did exactly that. She prepped for everything and left nothing to chance. Lo and behold, she got the job! Fast forward to three years later, when she was ready for her career next steps, she had a whole slew of tech companies interested in having her on their team.

That said, there's still an emotional component to pivoting - especially when it's unplanned. Sometimes you're forced to pivot due to circumstances beyond your control, leading to real and raw feelings of inadequacy and low self-esteem. It's normal to wonder "Why did this happen to me? Am I good enough? Is my work even valued?"

Again, this is the time to engage your support system. These are the people who remind you of your accomplishments and the value that you bring. They will help you see outside of the current situation and support you as you get back on your feet.

As mentioned previously, you should also leverage your support system to identify new opportunities. Let as many people as possible in your network know the types of roles you're looking for, the types of industries you want to be in, the types of problems you can solve.

You may have to cast a wider net and expand your search to more industries and positions. You have to give yourself the best chance of success by opening yourself up to new opportunities so you can continue forward on your journey.

If you find yourself taking an unplanned pivot, remember to draw on your support system and reach out to your network because they'll support you in your time of need.

In the beginning of this chapter, I mentioned the quote """Don't compare your 'behind the scenes' with someone else's highlight reel". That advice is especially relevant when you find yourself making an unplanned pivot. Remember that your career roadmap won't always be linear, so focus on what you can control and let everything else fall into place.

Key Takeaways

- **Leading Without Authority**: You don't need a title to be a leader. A leader inspires others to be their best. Sharing best practices and helping team members not only boosts overall team performance, it positions you as a team collaborator.
- **Managing Up, Down, and Across**: Managing subordinates is the most straight forward management relationship. Managing up means you're aligning your goals with your superiors.

Managing across is when you help peers by sharing best practices and providing support on critical tasks that they may need help on. It's critical to cultivate each of these skills as you activate your leadership journey.

- **Managing Setbacks**: Everyone has setbacks, even if you can't see them. I didn't get jobs that I wanted in my career, and that's ok. Setbacks and failures are normal, the key is to learn from them. Sometimes setbacks force you to pivot, and that can open other doors for you.

6

PARTNERSHIP

I was one year into my role at SAP when people approached me saying "Hey, Maggie, as you think about what's next, you should consider serving on boards." I hadn't thought about it before then, but even though I was focusing on my role, I found myself intrigued by the idea. The seed was planted.

A Board is the governing body of a company consisting of a group of individuals known as the Board of Directors. Collectively, they represent the shareholders of the company. The Board of Directors are usually former or current C-level executives or thought leaders in business or academics, each bringing decades of experience into the boardroom. As part of their responsibilities, they hire (and sometimes fire) the CEO, assess the company's strategic direction and performance, and advise the CEO and the management team.

In recent years, the spotlight has been shone on gender and ethnic diversity on boards. Since more than 70% of consumer spending is influenced by women, it only makes sense to have diverse and inclusive leaders at all levels of the organization – starting from the very top. The board of directors needs to be a representation of the people that they're selling to which helps explain why the state of California, the NASDAQ exchange, and the FTSE in London are requiring boards of directors to be more diverse and inclusive.

About a year after that conversation at SAP, I was invited to attend a private panel discussion about women on boards, in a very chic loft in New York City. When I entered, I was greeted by the organizers and a room of 30 other senior female executives from a variety of companies. We sat in a half circle, close to each other, eager to hear from two very seasoned board directors about their own journey getting on their first board and experience as board directors.

They first shared their impressive backgrounds as operating executives in Fortune 500 companies. They shared their learnings in serving on boards in various stages of a company's lifecycle. But the most interesting part to me was how challenging it was for them to get on their first board. One executive shared that it took her 18 months to land her first board. They gave us plenty of advice to prepare ourselves for boards, from crystallizing our desired boards, to crafting our own individual value proposition, and how best to leverage our network.

I sat there intently listening to them and taking lots of notes. It felt like I was exposed to a whole new world. Of course, when I was at Level 3 and SAP, I interacted with our board of directors but thinking of myself as one of these board directors was a foreign concept to me.

As I learned more, I knew that this would be the next step for me one day. In many ways, preparing myself for a board role was not that different from an operating role. I needed to develop a value proposition for myself that would show-case my expertise and experiences.

For example, I always think about my core value prop as a tech executive specializing in business and brand transfor-mation, cloud computing and someone who's passionate about diversity and inclusion. My time working at ADIC, Sun Microsystems, Microsoft, Level 3, and SAP was marked by rapid transition and growth, so I would use some of the initiatives with quantifiable outcomes as my proof points. Having spent 20 years in the tech sector, I knew that I wanted to serve on the board of other tech companies one day.

CRAFTING YOUR VALUE PROPOSITION

As you're fostering your sponsorship relationship, it helps to create a concise elevator pitch about yourself and where you're heading. By doing so, your sponsor would know how best to leverage your strengths and experience to support your career growth.

Maybe your sponsor has worked with you for a long time and knows you well. For me, that person was Allison at Microsoft. She knew me based on our working relationship. Or maybe you're new to the organization and your sponsor doesn't know you very well, in which case it's up to you to communicate your value proposition for yourself. Either way, crafting a value proposition helps clarify your exper-tise and your intentions.

My advice is to think deeply about who you are and the value you add. Think deeply about your aspirations. Think deeply about what you care about and what you're good at. Think about what you want to learn. Think about the industries or functions you excel in. Think about the value you provide to your sponsor. Above all, be very specific about it.

In our Women's Sponsorship programs, we ask protégés to list out three to five things that they want their sponsor to know about them in their first sponsorship meeting. Three is best because anything more than that is hard to remember. It's even better to back them up with stories or proof points that paint a clear picture of who you are and the value you offer to a team.

ALIGNING YOUR GOALS

Going back to my first job out of college, it didn't have anything to do with the internet or the cloud. It didn't have anything to do with marketing either. I was a junior buyer in the purchasing department at a fast-growing data storage company, not unlike today's hyper-growth startups. It wasn't my dream job; that would have been marketing. But it did get my foot in the door, a job to pay my bills. And it gave me a chance to prove myself. Little did I know, I had stumbled into the tech industry at the beginning of a multi-decade boom.

For a tech company with about a hundred employees when I joined, ADIC had a kind and gentle culture. It was a culture in which people had each other's backs. A place where people worked hard and often played hard together. Starting from CEO Peter van Oppen, he always addressed everyone in his company-wide meetings as team members. To this day, I still address my teams as team members. In the purchasing department we were like a small family.

Peter Hews, my first boss, was a great boss. He had a stern face and a reputation as a tough negotiator. I remember some people in other departments and suppliers saying they were scared of him. But those of us who got to know Peter, recognized the loving family man he is. He took really good care of his team and treated us all like family.

At the time, my job meant everything to me. I worked really, really hard, often over weekends if I had to. I may not have had the experience that my colleagues had, but I did have one powerful advantage. While they all had families and interests outside of work, I did not. For me, work was everything. I would work nights and come in on weekends. I made sure that whatever needed to be done, was done as quickly as possible.

I'm not suggesting that you should do this. It just worked for me at the time. I've always been an overachiever. I felt very uncomfortable when I didn't get to work on complex challenges. Even in my twenties, I spent my leisure time reading BusinessWeek. Recently, I've been mentoring a talent, an immigrant from India, who's in her early twenties who is the same way. She works non-stop and still feels like she needs to find ways to be more efficient. To her, work is a joyful challenge. She asked me, "Do you think I'm crazy? I'm crazy, right?" I laughed, and said, "Yep, you're absolutely crazy, but that's ok. I was the same way when I was at your age."

I worked so hard because I love learning new things. Plus, I had nothing to lose. I was more open to taking risks and to thinking outside of the box. In fact, I didn't even know there was a box. There was nothing to prevent me from trying something new. So when I had the idea to save money with offshore manufacturing for some of the core components we purchased to build our tape backup library products, I just went for it. In working closely with our Engineering department, we lowered the cost of our cable components by a staggering 70%. Our COO at the time told me that it represented savings of a penny a share. From his facial expression, I knew it was significant for the company.

But I still wanted to be in marketing, so when Dorothy, a friend of mine in the marketing department, told me that the hiring manager of a recently opened junior product manager position suggested that I apply, I jumped on it. I was super excited because this was going to be my ticket to get into marketing. Since the hiring manager indirectly invited me to apply, I thought it was my position to lose.

I interviewed for the role and *was so sure* that I got the job. After the interview process, I was told by the hiring manager that I was great, but they decided to go with another candidate. It was soul-crushing, but what he said next made it ten times worse. He added that they felt I was "overqualified" for the job.

"Overqualified?!?!" I couldn't believe what I had heard. "How could I be overqualified if I've never even worked in marketing?!?" I thought to myself.

I remember talking to my manager, Peter, about what had just happened. I was overcome with emotion and tears were dropping. Little did I know, he went to the CEO of the company and told him what happened.

I was shocked. ADIC was a relatively small company at the time, but I never had a direct conversation with the CEO. I never anticipated that my manager would go directly to the CEO. I was a hard worker, but I was still a junior employee, fresh out of college, who was looking to leave his team no less! Looking back, I could not have asked for a better sponsor. Peter used his political capital to help me grow my then nascent career.

Now that the meeting between myself and Peter van Oppen (we called him PVO), the CEO was scheduled, I was nervous, but simultaneously excited and grateful. I didn't need to tell him what happened because he already knew. PVO proceeded to tell me I was a valued team member, and that he had no doubt more openings were on the horizon. I was still in my early twenties and getting rejected for the junior marketing position felt like an end to my marketing career, before it even began. I'm sure Peter could sense that I was feeling defeated. He then said, "Maggie, the next job that opens up in marketing is yours."

Even with PVO's commitment and support, I was still a little skeptical and didn't think anything of it. This was my first job out of college, so I just thought that when a hiring manager asks you to interview for a position, the job is yours. I didn't know that when they asked you to interview, that means that other people may have been asked to interview too. I may have had an advantage, but that was no guarantee that I'd get the job.

I also learned that when one door closes another one opens. A few months later, another opportunity came up in marketing. This time, it wasn't a junior product manager, it was an actual product manager position, meaning it was a level higher than the position I was "overqualified" for.

I applied for the job and went through all the interviews. To not take any chances, I also ensured PVO is aware that I threw my hat in the ring for the job. This time, I got the job! PVO congratulated me and said that I earned the spot all on my own. I don't know if the CEO's promise had anything to do with it, but I was thrilled.

Not everyone will have the CEO advocating for you. But everyone has the power to go above and beyond and align their professional goals to their managers' goals. I was very fortunate that my boss sponsored me to get into marketing, but I earned that privilege. I worked my tail off to showcase my commitment and the values I bring to the company. Even though I didn't get the first marketing job that I applied for, my reputation within the company earned me an eventual position in marketing.

Another thing I learned along the way in my career is that you also need to take your managers on your career journey. When a manager is surprised by your career move, you may burn a bridge. I admit that it is a fine line between being communicative of your career aspirations that may take you outside of your immediate group, and not surprising your chain of command when it's time to move on. It depends on how strong your relationship is with your manager and how supportive your manager is in your career growth. I've had managers who were mad at me for leaving their groups to pursue a different role. But don't let that stop you. The most important thing is that you're at peace with your decision.

The moral of the story is to focus on what's in your control and enroll people to sponsor you based on your work ethic, your experiences, and your reputation. Good managers will appreciate your effort and cheer for you, even if it means that you end up leaving their team.

ABOVE AND BEYOND

I was fortunate enough to work with many great managers in my career, but a question that often comes up when I tell these stories is "That's great Maggie, but what if your boss is apathetic and doesn't care about your success?" I had been there too and had my fair share of managers who I didn't connect with. In that case, they may be your manager, but they aren't your ideal sponsor. I'd suggest you go find someone who believes in you.

When I think of my sponsors throughout my career, nobody came out and said, "Hey, I'm going to be your sponsor" except Allison at Microsoft. It was an organic partnership, born out of mutual respect, and my work ethic and willingness to align my goals to my sponsor, whether it was my manager, or a leader within another department. Your sponsors will believe in you and advocate for you because you've taken the time to understand their goals and help them achieve them. This organizational alignment is what drives results for the business. You will have demonstrated your commitment, capacity, and competence - in return your leaders will go out of their way to support your growth by giving you visibility and expanded responsibilities within the organization.

It's not that they're doing you any favors either - you've proven your worth and added immense value to the business and the company. That makes people say "Yes, I'm willing to use my political capital to help you advance your career." By taking on bigger responsibility, it's a win for the sponsor, a win for the team, and a win for the company.

THE SHOULDER TAP

At Tenshey, I've had the privilege of working with so many ambitious women growing their careers. Through our Women Sponsorship programs, we spend a lot of time helping mid-career women find sponsors so they can grow within their current company. In the pre-pandemic period, the program included an in-person workshop.

Our team of coaches usually lead these workshops, but I used to still attend, especially in the early days. To be able to witness the lightbulb moments these leaders have in reaching their career goals is food for the soul. I still do a fireside chat with every cohort in our sponsorship program to share my own stories and learnings in my journey to the C-suite. One day we were facilitating a workshop for a client and the client added an executive panel as part of the program. The client executives shared their own sponsorship experiences, how they started their careers, and how they ended up in their current roles.

The common thread woven through all their stories was that they all had mentors or sponsors tap them on the shoulder and ask them to take on a new opportunity. When they were done speaking, they opened the conversation up for questions.

I remember a Black woman who was sitting in the front of the room raised her hand and stood up, ready to ask her question. I was sitting in the back of the room observing. I could tell she was a bit nervous. She started by saying "I need your help!" She then continued, her voice cracking, trying to fight back tears in her eyes, "I really love hearing all your stories, and I appreciate it. At the same time, people who look like me don't get tapped on the shoulder."

The entire room fell silent. You could feel the tension in the air. It was a powerful moment that sent a shockwave through the room.

Right then one of the executives on the panel, a white man, said "You know what, Lisa? I'm going to give you my cell phone number. Call me any time. I'll be your sponsor." All of a sudden, other attendees rallied around her and said "You know, Lisa, I have worked with you. I know how amazing you are. The great thing is that you're in this program. You're going to get visibility."

Towards the end of the day, I walked over to her. I tapped her on the shoulder, no pun intended, and said "Hey Lisa, I'm Maggie. I'm the CEO of Tenshey, which put this sponsorship program together with your company. I would love to mentor you. If you're open to it, let's have a call, and take it from there."

I later found out that two out of the three executives on the panel reached out to her, and the executive who gave her his phone number ended up meeting with her frequently. He gave her pointers and helped her open doors to new opportunities.

I also continued to work with her periodically. I've learned that Lisa is a wife, and a mom of two adorable children. During our calls, I'd ask how her sponsorship program was going and what opportunities she was looking at. One of the great benefits of mentoring or sponsoring others is that I learn as much, if not more, as the mentees or protégés learned from me. Speaking to her opened my eyes even more because it helped me understand the challenges she faced as a Black woman and as a mother – especially during the COVID-19 pandemic, and a period of intense social injustice.

Through Lisa, I learned a few things. First, I learned that women routinely underestimate their transferable skills. Before the program, Lisa thought that the only way she could move up was that her manager would get a promotion or move to a new role. That might be true if she was in a small business, but she was in a Fortune 500 company, with a gigantic workforce. The program opened her eyes to potential opportunities that can utilize her broad skillset.

Second, I learned that remote workers (pre-pandemic) believed that their upward mobility is limited because they didn't work at the headquarters office. I would say that it is true to a certain extent, usually due to lack of visibility and advocacy. There is this perception of "out of sight, out of mind". But with sponsorship, capable talents gain both visibility and advocacy, and can even thrive as much as those who work full time in the office.

In one of our recent Women Sponsorship programs, we had a cohort of women who were all remote workers. They'd always worked from their home offices, even before the pandemic. We've seen a significantly higher rate of promotions and role expansions due to sponsorship. The post-pandemic shift to remote or hybrid work actually levels the playing field a bit as a majority of the workplace has experienced working remotely and managing virtual work teams.

Third, I learned that while we may all have our career aspirations, the degree of risks we could afford to take varies. I used to wonder why people don't take bigger risks in their career. I've taken risks in my career, from working on emerging and unproven products, to relocating to different states and companies. But that wasn't so difficult when both my husband and I were working professionals with no kids except Charlie, our Miniature Poodle. When you are the breadwinner of a family and you also have to balance your professional work and home duties, there's only so much risk you can tolerate.

Sure enough, by the end of the program, Lisa had been interviewed for a few positions and eventually found a new role within the company. She gained visibility within the organization and was poised for more growth because of it.

And, there's more. While I was visiting my family in Seattle, 18 months since my last visit due to COVID-19, I got a text from Lisa who said she had some good news to share. When we spoke, she told me that she got the promotion she has always wanted. She was beaming. She shared the story of how she got not just one, but two internal offers from two different groups within her company. We reminisced about her journey from that executive panel during our sponsorship program almost 2 years prior where she coura-geously raised her hand, to her now saying to me, "Maggie, I finally feel what it's like to be tapped on the shoulder." I was overjoyed for Lisa. Her hard work and tenacity have finally paid off.

As illustrated in many publicly available studies, women simply don't advance into leadership at nearly the same rate as their male colleagues do. It's even worse for women of color. When people say, "I got tapped on the shoulder for my role." That's not everyone's experience, which is why organizations need to be so deliberate with fostering spon-sorship.

PARTNERING UP

During my fireside chat with our sponsorship program members, I emphasize that it's their responsibility to convey their value proposition to their sponsor. I explain the importance of clearly conveying your goals, but also understanding how your unique blend of skills and experi-ences helps your sponsor so you can work in partnership with each other. A successful partnership is based on trans-parency about where you want to go, where you need help, and the value you provide.

I also suggest that you communicate with your sponsor often. One of the most common statements I hear is that "My sponsor is a busy executive, they don't have the time. I don't want to bother them." My response is that everybody has time to read a two-sentence email. Don't write a long email, just a short email saying, "Thank you for your time. Here are the key things that I took away from it. And this is what I'm working on."

I can tell you from first-hand experience, sponsors love to hear about your progress. Let's say you were introduced to someone by your sponsor and a conversation about career opportunities; after that conversation, send a quick note to your sponsor saying, "Thank you so much for that introduction. I had a great conversation, and we will meet again for a specific opportunity."

Your sponsor wants to know that their efforts are impactful. Telling them what happened strengthens the relationship and makes them aware of the progress you're making. They'll know that you're coachable, and that you're taking advantage of the opportunities they're providing you.

BUILD SPONSORSHIP MUSCLES

Building partnership is one thing, but sustaining that relationship is another thing. At this point, you've already aligned your goals with your sponsor. You've even acted on your sponsor's feedback. Now it's about having an ongoing dialogue with her on how to continue to advance her goals while simultaneously advancing your career.

In an example of how sponsorship is a partnership, one pair of sponsor-program members in one of our Women Sponsorship programs with a Fortune 100 healthcare company stood out for me. Nyla, a program member, worked in the marketing department. She was selected by her company to participate in our sponsorship program, which meant that she was already a high-potential employee. When she first started in the program, she was engaged in all the learning events, devoured the content, and created a plan to find a sponsor that would help advance her career.

Nyla did some sleuthing and came up with a list of potential sponsors that could help get her the visibility she needed to grow. Not only had she done her homework, she was strategic about who she approached for sponsorship.

Now that she had a list of potential sponsor candidates, she started approaching them one by one, explaining why she wanted a "skip level" sponsor through a short presentation she prepared. She eventually had a conversation with Bree, a highly esteemed marketing executive within the company.

Nyla made her case and demonstrated the "Three Cs" of commitment, capacity, and competency that I spoke about earlier in this book. Having the courage to approach a senior leader and have a candid conversation showed commitment to her own growth and a capacity to take on more challenges made an impression on Bree, so she agreed to sponsor Nyla.

Bree took her role as a sponsor very seriously. She offered Nyla bi-weekly calls, an opportunity that even Bree's direct reports didn't typically have. Based on Nyla's career aspirations, Bree recommended other leaders within the company that Nyla should connect with. She told Nyla that when she reached out to those leaders, let them know Bree sent her - further bolstering Nyla's visibility and credibility within the organization. In other words, if Bree was willing to endorse Nyla, she *must* be good. The most interesting thing about their relationship is that Bree led a different part of the organization, so she exposed Nyla to an entirely new set of people, people that she never would have had access to without connections.

Prior to joining the sponsorship program, Nyla never would have thought of approaching a skip-level manager, but now she's having bi-weekly calls and making a name for herself within the organization. As a result, she had told us that she made more progress in her career in the past few months than she has in the past several years.

When it comes to "building the muscles", she's been referring back to the Women's Sponsorship learning events and reaching out to other people in the organization with the same organizational capital as Bree. She's actively building relationships with VP level leaders and up leveling her skills and competencies so that she can add value to those individuals. She's building her confidence and advocating for herself, volunteering for new nationwide marketing campaigns that are rapidly growing her reputation within the company.

Now she has the confidence and skills to approach executives and position herself as an asset to the organization. Rather than limiting herself to the day to day of her own job, she's aligning her goals with her sponsors and with the broader organization. And it's paying off nicely for her. Nyla also gained a better understanding of how different groups interlock with each other to deliver organizational success.

When speaking to her, she emphasized the difference between a mentor and a sponsor. The first person she chose to sponsor her didn't meet the qualifications of a sponsor. She could offer career advice, but wasn't in a position to advocate for her for career advancement. Understanding the difference between a mentor and a sponsor helped her focus on leaders that could offer the upward visibility she was looking for.

For Bree, she felt it was both a pay-it-forward and a responsibility for her to be a sponsor. She recognized that she has been sponsored officially and unofficially throughout her career and she wouldn't be where she is now without that. She wanted to do just that for others. She also noted that when she looked at the top of the company, there was still very little diversity. She felt it was her responsibility as a leader to expand the leadership pipeline with more women.

Building a sponsorship partnership is like building muscle. It takes time, effort, repetition, and dedication to do it right. In our context, that means first and foremost, the ability to identify your sponsors, then having conversations with your sponsors that move the needle. That means getting their feedback on your current performance. That may mean getting their support to expand your horizon. Underpinning that all is the skill to enroll them into *wanting* to help you take your career to the next level - and that's what I mean when I say you have to build your "muscles".

It's a skill that you refine over time. You don't want to bombard them with conversations about your career, but try to have one conversation each quarter about your career growth to keep the momentum going.

GENTLE NUDGES

A conversation about your career growth doesn't have to be an overt request. Oftentimes, a subtle question about your own skill sets is all you need to get great feedback. You could ask about the experiences you need to gain to excel even more in your current role, or to better prepare you for your next role. You could showcase the abilities you've developed or the accomplishments you've had in the time since you've last met with them.

You may not have these conversations every quarter - and that's ok. I had times when I didn't need to discuss my career growth with my sponsors, but it was intentional. I knew what skill I was working on, or I knew that my sponsors were already advocating for me, so I didn't need to bring it up myself. The point is that I was intentional about it. That allowed me to develop my functional and technical skills while still making sure that I'm still working on the long-term goal of growing my career.

I can tell you from first-hand experience that so many women just don't prioritize these conversations. I've seen women place so much emphasis on doing such a great job that they forget to prioritize their career growth. I've seen highly skilled women, whether they're in sales, or engineering, or marketing, focusing solely on developing their functional skills. They'll take another programming class. They'll register for a marketing conference. Or they'll enroll in a class at the local community college – all of which increases their proficiency in their current role. But then they were frustrated that they had not seen the career growth they expected. That's why I say it's equally important to develop leadership, collaboration skills, and advocacy from your sponsors to help position you for growth.

On the flip side, you may find that your sponsor simply isn't advocating for you as much as you'd like. You're putting in the work and doing your part as the protégé, but your sponsor isn't using their political capital to expose you to other opportunities in the organization. In that case, you have to figure out where the disconnect is. Maybe your sponsor is under a lot of stress in their own role and hasn't had the time to give you the exposure you need. Another instance I've seen is where your sponsor doesn't feel you're quite ready for the next level yet, or that there may be a misaligned perception of what you can handle.

Developing the muscle of tactfully checking in with your sponsor every quarter is helpful in each of these scenarios. Sometimes a gentle reminder is all they need to introduce you to another executive of a great team. Maybe having a mature conversation about your capacity to take on more responsibility will get you the visibility you want. Or that you need to circle back and demonstrate the progress you've made to help advance their goals. Usually that's enough to get things back on track. If not, it's time to start looking for other sponsors within the organization.

WHY YOU NEED MULTIPLE SPONSORS

That underscores the importance of having multiple sponsors. Whenever people ask me if they should look for multiple sponsors within an organization, I always respond with a resounding "Yes!"

Sometimes, you just won't get the visibility and support that you were expecting from your sponsor. It may not be your fault, and honestly, it may not even be their fault. In most cases, especially if you're working in an organization that's big enough, you will likely be working with multiple teams, and multiple leaders on multiple projects across different business units. In that case, you have a prime opportunity to align your goals to a variety of sponsors.

If you remember my time at Microsoft, I had Allison as a sponsor who focused on the marketing side of the house. But I also had Phil, who oversaw the overall P&L side of the cloud business, who was just as important of a sponsor for me. I aligned my goals to theirs, and in return they each advocated and found opportunities for me.

There will also be adversity. You'll be turned down for jobs. Sponsors will leave the company, or worse, lose their political capital within the company due to dreaded "reorgs". This happens quite often with mergers and acquisitions or when a company is re-prioritizing their focus areas. Growing up in tech, one thing I've learned is that people change jobs often. They'll often change jobs within the same company, or within the same industry. Not to mention, cases of organizational shakeups, which happen all the time.

Remember I mentioned Fred, one of my managers at Microsoft who was also my sponsor? When he moved into the Business Applications business unit, I lost him a sponsor (but gained a mentor). Sometimes you'll have managers that you don't connect with or that you work in a hostile organization and won't receive support from leaders. That's why it's so important to cultivate relationships with multiple sponsors across the organization.

CELEBRATE SUCCESSES, BIG OR SMALL

One of the questions I get about fostering the sponsorship relationship is how often one should communicate with their sponsors outside of their scheduled meetings. One of the best ways to keep communication going in between your meetings is to celebrate your successes along the way. That also means celebrating your sponsor's successes and creating an environment where they can celebrate yours.

Your sponsor shouldn't just know when you get a new role. They should know when you had a great meeting with someone they introduced you to within the organization. They should know about new skills that you've acquired and new responsibilities that you've taken on.

My suggestion is to communicate and celebrate these types of successes with your sponsor as they occur, but to keep it brief, given most of your sponsors are busy executives. Sharing these little accomplishments strengthens the relationship and shows that you're serious about your career.

Let's say one of your sponsors connected you with someone in the organization to explore a different opportunity. After you had that conversation, it would be great to send a quick message to your sponsor thanking them for the connection, letting them know how great of a conversation it was. You could even fill them in on next steps - all of which show that you're taking advantage of the opportunities your sponsor is providing you. It's part of building that communication muscle with your sponsor and strengthening that relationship.

When I was at SAP, I was a sponsor for Marsha in my group. Marsha is a career marketer with a CPG (consumer packaged goods) background. Marsha was ready to grow and wanted to move into people management, so I suggested that she connect with different business units as well as different parts of Marketing. I wanted her to get a sense of how each of the teams worked, discover where her interests are, and scope out potential opportunities for herself.

After she spoke to one of the groups that I recommended to her, she sent me a quick email saying, "Hey Maggie, thanks so much for the connection. I had a great conversation with that leader over there. And they're actually opening a new role that I'm planning to apply for."

I said, "Great! Keep me posted." That brief email showed that my feedback and my guidance mattered, and it also helped keep Marsha top of mind for me, along with many other priorities on my mind. I saw that Marsha was serious about her career and took action. When she ended up applying for the job and becoming one of the final candidates for the role, she sent me another note asking if I could send an email to the hiring manager recommending her, which I enthusiastically did. And when she emailed me again to let me know that she ended up getting the job, that made my day!

I share that story to say that the sponsor protégé relationship is a two-way street - Marsha expressed interest in growing and worked hard, and I used my organizational capital to help her get the job she deserved. At the end, it was Marsha who showcased her capabilities to land the job. As a sponsor, I merely open doors for conversations. Helping capable talents to continue to grow their career is a way to increase organizational capability and retain talents.

TRANSITIONING FROM PROTÉGÉ TO SPONSOR

Up to this point I've been talking about the importance of the protégé building the muscle of communication with the sponsor. At some point, as you advance through your career, you'll find yourself in a position to be able to sponsor others. It's an exciting transition because now you've accumulated your own organizational capital and can expose others to opportunity. In fact, I believe it's our duty as leaders to pay it forward and give others the support and visibility they deserve. Paying it forward has been the top reason many of the sponsors in our programs chose to sponsor someone in their company.

When I was at Level 3 Communications, I saw myself having three sponsors. They included my direct manager, who was the president of North America, the Chief Human Resources officer and the Global Chief Marketing Officer. I had the unique honor of aligning my goals to each of their goals, but I also found myself in a position to sponsor others.

My responsibility then was to grow the North American business under the North America President, which meant I had the opportunity to give visibility to my direct reports. I was responsible for aligning our regional marketing initiatives with the global initiatives under the Global CMO. Lastly, working with the CHRO, I used my passion for diversity and inclusion to advance the company's overall Diversity and Inclusion goals by pioneering the first group mentorship program for women at Level 3 - a program that led to my nomination by our CHRO for the Woman of the Year award by the Rocky Mountain Chapter of Women in Cable Telecommunications.

As a senior executive, I had the opportunity to sponsor more talents, especially women, giving them visibility and exposure within the organization via the political capital that I had built. That's what makes me most proud of my time there - the fact that I was able to not only advance my own career via sponsorship, but to advance others' careers.

By the time I left Level 3, three of my direct reports threw their hats in the ring as my successor. They were all capable leaders with their unique experiences and superpowers. In the end, I was very pleased to see that one of them succeeded me for the role.

As I grew as an executive, I gained an appreciation for the importance of succession planning and creating a legacy. As the saying goes 'A rising tide lifts all boats' - the power of lifting others up so that you can continue to reach new heights.

As a growing executive, it's in your best interest to build a succession pipeline across the organization to minimize business disruption. Whether that means sponsoring someone directly underneath you, someone a few levels below, or someone in a completely different part of the organization.

I'm a champion of diversity and inclusion and recommend that you identify talent across the entire spectrum of diversity, whether that's diversity in functional skills, diversity in terms of experience, diversity in terms of gender, race, ethnicity, religion, education, etc. Throughout my career, I've been very intentional about cultivating that diversity and sponsoring people that are different from me. By doing so, I gained broader perspectives and that the business can benefit more with a diverse workforce.

EVERYONE'S JOURNEY IS UNIQUE

It's common to look at other people's journey and say, "Wow, this person had such an amazing career. I wish I could do what they have done." But I always remind people that at the end of the day, everyone has different experiences. We have different upbringings, different challenges, and different environments, all of which influence the decisions we make.

My advice is to not get too hung up on what someone else has done. Don't beat yourself up if you don't get the promotion you want. Even worse, don't assume that you're deficient in any way. Like the phrase I shared previously, "Never compare your 'behind the scenes' to someone else's highlight reel." Comparing yourself to others is the fastest way to feel depressed and unmotivated in your career. It's so much more productive to focus on your own journey and create your own success recipe.

I mentioned my friend Brian Reaves from SAP, who has most recently become the Chief Belonging, Diversity and Equity at UKG. Brian started his career as an engineer. Brian was a brilliant engineer with a long and successful career in tech, and he's Black. At first glance, it looks like a major shift to go from engineering to the head of Belonging,

Diversity, and Equity, but when you look deeper, it was an easy pivot with a lot of parallels.

People often ask about how he transitioned from being an engineer to a C-suite executive in the diversity and inclusion area for some of the world's most prestigious brands, and he had some very insightful things to say.

I found Brian's approach very interesting. When I asked about his pivot from engineering to diversity and inclusion he told me, "Instead of pivoting from engineering to diversity, equity, and inclusion, it was more about bringing an engineering and an innovative mindset to what I think is one of the most complex business challenges that needs to be addressed. I just don't do it by writing code anymore." Brian applied his core problem solving skills set to a completely different business problem.

As I learned about his career journey, he shared how he started off as an individual contributor like everyone else. He shared with me, "My focus was really on becoming an expert in what I was doing. In that case, it was software engineering, based on my degrees in math and computer science." Early in his career he was able to master a few mainframe languages so he could write the most efficient code possible. As he advanced in his career, he pursued his interest in optimizing databases and extracting insights from the data.

As his career grew and he took on leadership roles, he honed a set of techniques to impart his skills to others. As he built his technical acumen, he simultaneously honed his leadership and communication capabilities. The more I got to know him, the more I appreciate Brian's core skill in his ability to solve big problems. Whether they were engineering problems or people problems, he was solving problems that had a tremendous impact on people's careers.

As he grew into management, he led larger and more diverse teams. He went on to share that "All along that professional arc, when I was trying to understand how best to lead people, I started to see differences in people's skill sets. There was an art as well as a science to how you blend people that have different backgrounds and experiences. For me, coming from a socio-economically challenged background, I started focusing on 'How can I be the best leader? How do I bring together people with different skills and varying backgrounds so that they can work together and be most successful?" Those questions prepared him for the belonging, diversity, equity, and inclusion work that he champions now.

As he took on more responsibility and had more autonomy, he was able to put people in positions where he knew they would thrive. When I first met him at SAP, he was still in an engineering role, but he had refined his "side hustle" of integrating diverse talent into high-performing teams. He was so good at it, that he eventually got the opportunity to formally execute his approach first as the Head of Diversity and Inclusion of the CEO Board Area for SAP, then as the Chief Diversity and Inclusion Officer at Dell.

When I look at my own career, I look at it in terms of my "act one" and my "act two". "Act one" was about growing my marketing career and becoming the Chief Marketing Officer of a tech company. But at its core, being in tech, my focus was still to solve big problems. Now, in the entrepreneurial "act two" of my career, like Brian, I'm solving the problem of diversity and inclusion and even more importantly, belonging and equity, which is what guided my decision to found Tenshey, my leadership acceleration company - and ultimately to write this book.

My focus now is to help organizations accelerate diverse talents' growth. As you progress in your career, you'll find out that they're things that you absolutely love to do and things that you are just wildly passionate about. You allow your passion to direct your career and the lifestyle you want to build for yourself.

That's why I feel so strongly that people should periodically check in with themselves and ask "Is this still the plan that I want to be on? Do I still want to go down this path? Is this path leading me to what I ultimately want to do?" And an even more important and elusive question, "does it make me happy?"

Just like a business plan or workout program, to achieve your desired outcome, it's not something that you create once and tuck away in a corner, it's something that you must implement, actively pursue, and frequently adjust. You have to adapt and iterate based on what you want to do and have the courage to take chances and believe in yourself. I'm not talking about taking reckless risks, I'm talking about leaning on your support system and making bold moves that get you where you want to go.

I think that punctuates the point about everyone's path being unique and that success isn't linear. Instead of getting down on yourself, figure out what you can learn from where you are on your journey.

Key Takeaways

- **Craft a Value Proposition**: Be clear about what makes you unique and communicate that. It's powerful to own your narrative.

- **Align Your Goals**: Once you've identified your sponsors, align your goals to theirs, assuming you're in the same business groups. It builds massive goodwill and will pay off in the long run.
- **Build the Muscles**: Master the art of communicating often, but concise with your sponsor. Share your successes and show them that you're acting on their advice. It's a skill that requires practice, and it builds that relationship.
- **Pay It Forward**: This chapter started with partnership with your sponsors and ended with you can sponsor with your protégés as you advance through your own career. Paying it forward is the number one reason leaders sponsor others.

7

WIN-WIN-WIN

In previous chapters, I introduced you to my good friend Brian Reaves. Not only was Brian a highly accomplished engineer turned DEI (Diversity, Equity, and Inclusion) executive, he understood the power of sponsorship and actively sponsored rising talent within the teams that he led.

One of the sponsorship stories Brian shared was of a young man named Julian. Brian met Julian in 2015 when he was still a student at Delaware State University. In those days, Brian led a program at SAP called "Project Propel" which focused on building a broader pipeline of Black and Hispanic talent via partnerships with historically black colleges.

He told me the story of a talk that he gave at DSU to a group of students when a young man named Julian asked him a few questions. Julian told him, "I'm not the best student here, but I have more grit than anybody and I'm willing to do whatever it takes to be successful if given the opportunity."

After that meeting, Brian agreed to mentor Julian and helped him get a foothold in the tech sector. Fast forward to the following year and Brian hired Julian onto his D&I team to scale Project Propel at SAP. His job was to build more relationships with historically black colleges and recruit a diverse talent pipeline - but Julian had different plans.

In their sponsorship conversations, Julian expressed that he wanted to take on a more technical role. Prior to leaving SAP for Dell, Brian, leveraging his own network, helped Julian secure a technical strategy role. It was a true success story of an influential tech leader recruiting and promoting young talent.

But the story didn't end there.

Brian and Julian continue to stay in touch; their sponsorship relationship turned into mentorship. Two years into his tenure at Dell, Brian had an opening on his team that would be a great fit for Julian and his expertise. After a few conversations, Julian joined Dell as a tech innovation strategist on his D&I team.

What I love about this story is that Brian and Julian have a great relationship that started when Julian was still in college and spanned across companies, where Brian advocated for Julian and gave him the visibility he needed to grow his career. Julian now has the political capital to advocate for himself - and even started paying it forward by sponsoring the next generation of talent.

When I asked what he thought about the process, Brian shared that "Sponsorship is an evolutionary relationship. Many times you put your reputation on the line for someone else. For me, it's important that I understand not only the goals and aspirations of that individual, but are they going to work as hard as I would expect myself to work in order to achieve what they want?"

Brian told me, "I saw a lot of myself, quite honestly, in Julian. Knowing that his background was very similar to mine. Now he's mentoring young people, giving them opportunities to do things in their life that in South Central Los Angeles, they would never have if they didn't know those things were possible."

I believe that diversity multiplies diversity. I've seen time and again that diverse leaders attract more diverse talents that follow their footsteps. You can't have inclusion without representation. In Julian and Brian's case, sponsorship was a win for Julian as the protégé, a win for Brian as the sponsor, and a win for both SAP and Dell as organizations.

When done right, sponsorship is that proverbial a win-win-win for all parties involved.

DANCING TO YOUR FAVORITE SONG

When it comes to diversity and inclusion in the workplace, it made me think of another gem that Brian Reaves imparted in one of our conversations.

He was quoting Verna Myers, the Harvard-trained lawyer, VP of Inclusion Strategy at Netflix, and famed TED speaker who created the phrase "Diversity is being invited to the party. Inclusion is being invited to dance."

To that end, Brian said "I was on a panel and we were talking about diversity, equity, inclusion, and belonging, and I think belonging is really important. When somebody asked me to describe the differences, I paid homage to Verna and said 'Diversity is being invited to the party. Inclusion is being asked to dance. And I added belonging is dancing to your favorite song. Equity is being asked to host the next party.' You know, you could be included, but never feel like you belong or were given equal opportunity to share your opinions."

That statement just touched my heart and sums up the critical role that sponsorship plays in fostering belonging, diversity, inclusion, and equity. I realized that my ascension to the C-suite in the male-dominated tech industry was rare and shouldn't be. I made it my mission to change that, but I had to make a convincing argument for it.

I've shared these stats earlier in this book but they're worth revisiting:

- According to McKinsey & LeanIn.Org's Women in the Workplace 2019 study, only 1 in 25 C-Suite executives is a woman of color. Corporations understand the need for greater Diversity, Equity, and Inclusion (DEI) in the workplace and yet, the needle has barely moved for women of color in senior executive positions.
- A 2020 study by the McKinsey Global Institute predicted an additional $12 trillion to the global GDP by 2025 by closing gender gaps in work and society in the public, private, and social sectors.
- McKinsey also predicted that gender balanced teams were 21% more likely to meet their profit goals than those that weren't
- The Workforce Diversity Network reported that organizations that prioritize Diversity and Inclusion had 39% higher customer satisfaction rates

Sponsorship, done intentionally to foster DEI, can be the mechanism to catalyze the transformational power of DEI to an organization.

THE "FROZEN MIDDLE" CHALLENGE

When we talk about the "frozen middle", we're talking about where people are getting stuck at levels to get into middle management, and therefore not being able to reach senior leadership positions. The frozen middle challenge is especially relevant to women who are mid-career professionals in the tech industry, and applies to other male-dominated industries. These are typically mid-career level managers or senior managers that are trying to break into the director level or equivalent.

We've seen that the higher you look in an organization, the more you see women and minorities fall off the map. Breaking into the director level is usually the first major obstacle, and it's hard enough to get there, but the higher up you go, the less likely you are to see women and minorities. This isn't just my personal observation, the annual Women in the Workplace study by McKinsey and Lean-In.org have demonstrated that for every 100 men promoted or hired into their first management position, only 72 women are given the opportunity to take the same step. And for every level all the way to the C-suite, the percentage of women getting promoted trails the male counterparts.

Companies have to be intentional about not just acknowledging this phenomenon, but trying to tackle it. I believe that fostering sponsorship is one of the most potent tools in the arsenal to do that.

As an employee, your functional skills come into play, but as you grow your career, your managerial skills, your leadership skills, your communication skills, your ability to gain visibility for yourself across the organization is what makes you a strong candidate for those positions. Having a strong sponsor who is willing to give you the insights and feedback you need, and simultaneously advocating for you are the differences between excelling in your career and staying stuck.

I've been fortunate enough to work in progressive companies that took DEI seriously. I've worked with managers and leaders that were vested in my success and exerted their influence to help me achieve my goals. But, as I spoke with some former colleagues and others through my work at Tenshey, I realize that my experience is not widely shared.

Women and minorities often face biases and have to deal with negative assumptions about their background and performance. It's not uncommon for your differences to work against you and shape people's perceptions of your work. To that end, I've seen people try to blend in and distance themselves from what makes them unique just so they fit in.

Brian Reaves had some very impactful insights to share regarding this. Rather than trying to fit in, he told me, "I have a responsibility to be my authentic self. I'm not the type of person that will come in and say 'I need to acquiesce and change to be like everybody else for me to be successful' because that's not expanding the aperture."

That was such a profound statement "that's not expanding the aperture" That's what DEI is about - it's about expanding the aperture so that companies can tap into the rich talents and viewpoints of their *entire* workforce - to advance the business. Sponsorship is a lever to make that happen.

He went on to talk about the challenges he faced as a Black man in tech by saying "We carry the weight of our intersection. If we fail, there are a bunch of people who are waiting for us to fail so that they can say, 'See, we tried, it doesn't work.' So we carry that, but I don't let it hold me back. My job is to ensure that isn't the norm. I can look around a room and see as many different intersections that I am in that room as well."

Modeling what worked for me in my own career journey, the specific women's sponsorship programs we created at Tenshey are designed to help women in what we call the "frozen middle" gain sponsorship from internal executives and leadership. In addition to coaching and peer to peer community support, they need senior leaders to open up their network, help them gain the visibility, and give them advocacy they need to break into those elusive management roles.

The results to date have been encouraging. We have seen close to 60% of participants in the programs reporting a progression in their career, including getting promotions, new roles, and expanded responsibilities within twelve months of the sponsorship program they are part of, compared to single digit numbers we typically see at this level in the tech industry. More advancements are expected as time goes on. This is how companies can have a chance to reach true diversity and inclusion.

GOING FOR THE WIN!

Sponsorship and a commitment to DEI isn't some fluffy, feel-good corporate initiative. It's a disruptive competitive advantage.

As a business executive, a passionate advocate of diversity, equity and inclusion, and a board of director of tech companies, I can say that DEI isn't a "favor" to "disadvantaged" employees, it is a business imperative.

By increasing investment into sponsorship, companies create a win-win-win for everyone involved. Sponsorship programs enhance organizational commitment to DEI, improve the company culture, and lead to financial gains.

Given the trend of protégés paying it forward and later becoming sponsors themselves, the companies involved will start to see a progression of diverse leadership in their pipeline, and fostering a sponsorship culture.

Sponsorship is a competitive advantage that benefits the organization, the individual sponsors, and the protégés.

It's a win for the company because it increases the number of women and minorities in the talent pipeline for growth. It helps with retention and progression in readiness of identified female leaders. And it empowered organizational commitment to diversity and inclusion.

It's a win for the sponsor because it aligns with organizational commitment to diversity and inclusion, increases leadership competencies by championing emerging leaders and increases the leader's personal and professional satisfaction as a sponsor of future leaders.

It's a win for the protégé because it strengthens their self-advocacy skills to support career advancement and growth. It provides greater visibility with access to senior leaders, and help overcome the glass ceilings and potential barriers to success

When done intentionally, sponsorship can boost retention, increase engagement, and add overall value to a company.

IT TAKES A VILLAGE

One of the things I love doing is to mentor the next generation executives as they blaze their trail into senior leadership.

I once received a message on LinkedIn, from a woman named Leslie, who asked if I could be her mentor. I didn't know Leslie personally, but she works at a company I'm very familiar with. When we spoke, she shared with me that becoming a CMO is her career north star and wanted to pick my brain.

I don't typically mentor people that I don't know because I believe that chemistry is a big part of the mentoring process. However, I was impressed by the time she took to research me, and her passion for marketing, all of which made an impression on me.

Leslie was the head of marketing for a business unit within the company. When we had our conversation over a video call, I realized that she was a driven, successful leader with high growth potential - so I agreed to mentor her. Nine months later, her manager, a C-level executive, was taking on another role within the company. Because of her stellar performance in driving the business, her manager, a sponsor of Leslie, recommended that she take on a larger role, to be responsible for both Sales and Marketing of that business unit.

It was a massive opportunity for her career, to have a P&L responsibility, and I was thrilled that she was in the running for the position. Leslie had a strong marketing background, and this role incorporated both sales and marketing would allow her to expand her skillset and had a direct responsibility of a revenue target. Another reason I was really excited for her was that while there is already a big gap in gender ratio at the executive level, the gap is even bigger in P&L roles.

It was a massive opportunity for her career, and I was thrilled that she was in the running for the position. But still, I knew that her career North Star was to eventually lead a marketing team as CMO, so I wasn't sure how she felt about the opportunity to oversee sales - and that she'll be reporting to another C-level executive in the company whom she hadn't established rapport with yet.

When the Head of People of the company reached out to me to ask my opinion of Leslie, I voiced my excitement and confirmed that she would be a great fit for this new challenge. On top of that, her manager, a well-respected executive who knew her well, was the one who recommended her for this expanded role.

A few weeks had passed by when I reached out to the Head of People to see if I could congratulate Leslie on her new role. To my surprise, she said, "Maggie, let's hold off for a bit because this is not a done deal. In fact, it would be helpful if you can help gauge her interest. This is a big role, we want to ensure she really wants this."

I know how hard it is for women to get leadership positions, especially a P&L role, *and* in tech. Leslie had a golden opportunity that would expand her capabilities and position herself for growth. At the same time, I reminded myself that she may not really want the job. So I decided to contact Leslie and find out for myself.

When I spoke with Leslie to gauge her interest in the position, she said "My manager recommended me for the job. I applied for it, but I also know one of my colleagues is also applying for the role. I don't know how this is going to go." I then probed further to get a sense of her interest for the role, "How do you feel about it?" She told me "Maggie, I'd really love it if I get this role. I just don't know if they think that I'm the right person for the role."

That's all I needed to hear.

I had a heart to heart with her and said, "Leslie, listen, if you really want this, which you do, you need to make it known to the hiring manager and showcase that you're the best person for this role. There should be no ambiguity about it." Leslie nodded, internalizing my advice and mapping out her next steps in the process. Leslie aced the interview and got offered the role. And not surprisingly, she was totally kicking-butt in the role and delivering growth for the company.

The moral of the story is that Leslie went through this entire process with a strong recommendation from her manager as her sponsor, with me as her mentor, and strong interest from the hiring manager and CHRO. And yet, there was still hesitation on her part because of the areas she had not had the experience to lead. This goes back to where women go for jobs only when they are 90-to-100% qualified while men go for jobs when they are 60% qualified. The missing ingredient was enthusiasm, backed by her own self confidence.

This story just underscores the point that it takes a village to achieve your goals, especially for women and even more so for women of color. Success isn't a solo endeavor fueled by sheer willpower and determination. Willpower and determination are important, but so are sponsors, mentors, coaches, and advocates - in other words, your support system.

I see a lot of cases where women just don't speak up for what they want. Even though they're extremely interested in something, they don't want to be seen as too eager. It's understandable. Like the story of Gail I shared earlier, some are afraid of being labeled "overly ambitious" which is rarely an issue for men.

People are not mind readers. If you are not explicit in your interest and enthusiasm, the other side may not think you're interested at all. Sometimes, it's also key to have a support system of sponsors and mentors to help you step out of your own shell and step into your power. You may just need gentle nudges along the way to remind you that you do belong and that you're more than good enough.

I sometimes wonder what would have happened if Leslie didn't have a strong sponsor and a company dedicated to advance diversity and inclusion, or if she didn't have advocates within the organization that wanted her to succeed. Sadly, this scenario plays itself out over and over again in companies across the country where bright, talented, hard working women miss out on great opportunities - and I've made it my life's work to change that, one leader at a time.

YOUR SPONSORS DON'T NEED TO LOOK LIKE YOU

One of the most common questions I get asked frequently is "Maggie, I really want my sponsor to be a woman, but there aren't any in leadership. What can I do?"

I think these questions are a different form of unconscious bias, and you're limiting yourself on your pool of potential sponsors. Rather than focusing on how your sponsor looks, the first question to ask yourself is, "How do I find a sponsor that I connect with?" When looking for sponsors, it's ideal to find people who know you as a person, a leader, someone who knows your work, so you can align your work to their goals. It doesn't matter what they look like, what gender they identify as, or where they come from. What matters is that they see your potential and that they feel compelled to help you.

If you look at tech, 80% of executive leaders are male. Finding a woman to sponsor you will be an uphill battle. If you think you need to reach out to other minorities or females as your sponsors, just imagine how many other people are thinking the same thing. And let's not forget, to thrive at the levels they are at, they are more inclined to perform better than their peers. Finding someone that you can align with is a better route to finding the best sponsor for you.

SPONSORSHIP IS NOT A FAVOR

One of my favorite things in our Women Sponsorship programs is to hear the stories from our members. We celebrate their successes and help problem-solve when they get stuck. One success story came from a product manager at a Global Tech company named Brenda. When Brenda first started our program, she struggled to identify multiple leaders as potential sponsors for her. She only had one person in mind, a VP of Product Management. It was ambitious, Brenda thought, because he was such a busy executive. But, she took her chances and approached him to be her sponsor.

Brenda had known this executive for several years and they had a working relationship, but after she learned about sponsorship, she officially initiated the protégé-sponsorship relationship with him. Brenda also noticed that through the program, her sponsor had evolved from a mentor to an official sponsor, bringing up her name when the opportunity arose.

Given their established trusting relationship, she felt comfortable opening up to him about how she was feeling within the organization. She made herself vulnerable and revealed that she felt like she had hit a ceiling and was considering leaving the company. It was an incredibly bold thing to do, but the response she got was shocking. Her sponsor asked her "Well Brenda, what do you want to do?"

She was flabbergasted. Rather than losing her job, her sponsor asked her what she'd like to do. Brenda didn't have an answer, but she knew that she wasn't happy where she was. Through the Women Sponsorship program, she used our "North Star Pyramid" to get really clear on what she liked to do and where she wanted to be in her career. During that process she realized that she loved product management, but wanted to be a people manager and be more involved on the strategy side of product management.

Once she told him that, he said "Let me make some phone calls. Are you ok with that?" Even then, Brenda wasn't sure she was going to stay with the company, but she was encouraged by her sponsor's actions, so he made calls to other senior executives within the department. His connections helped her eventually land a promotion to Director of Product Management.

Sponsorship was a huge win for Brenda because she was able to get her dream job without leaving the company. She is now on the strategy side of product management and leads a team. She also reports directly to the VP of another product line, whereas she used to report to a Senior Director. It was a win for the company because it aligns with their diverse leadership focus. And it was a win for her sponsor because he has made a direct impact for Brenda's career and helped the company to retain a great talent from leaving.

Had it not been for those honest conversations and him specifically asking her what she wanted to do, she would have left. It wasn't just about staying at her job, it was about finding a role that aligned with her North Star. Once she was clear on what she wanted, her sponsor was able to facilitate it and help make it happen.

PERFECT STRANGERS?

There will be times where a potential sponsor won't know you or your work very well; this is especially true in large organizations. That was certainly the case with Gail when I first heard of her. As the CMO of a 1,300-person team, it was almost impossible for me to know everyone one of my rockstar team members.

That's why defining your career North Star and crafting your value proposition are so important. They allow you to share the unique experiences and expertise you bring to the table, and to give others direction on how they can best help you. It goes without saying that your work ethic needs to speak for itself, but a well-defined North Star and value prop will do wonders for your career.

With the clarity of your value proposition and career North Star, a marvelous sponsor will do three key things for you. First, they may challenge you to set a broader vision for yourself, if they didn't think. Through my own experience working with sponsors and as a sponsor myself, sponsors have a broader view of opportunities across the organization and can push you to have a bigger vision for yourself.

I once spoke with a sponsor in one of Tenshey's women sponsorship programs whose protégé's goal was to become a director in the Fortune 100 company she works at. Her response to her protégé was "Why would you want to stop at that level? I want you to think further out" That kind of feedback is invaluable. Sometimes we need someone to have a broader view of the corporate world, and see more in us than we see in ourselves - a great sponsor will do just that.

Through the work we do at Tenshey, we've discovered that the highest probability for a successful sponsorship partnership is when a sponsor already knows the protégé and their work, and is willing to utilize their "political capital" to help the protégé grow their career. That said, there are always exceptions to the rules.

What if you're looking to branch out to a different function, a different part of the organization, or even a different company? In those cases, your potential sponsors may not know you or your work well. Those potential sponsors don't know you and can't judge how good of a protégé you'll end up being. It's a risky proposition because a sponsor puts their reputation on the line by endorsing and advocating for a protégé. That's why a protégé should demonstrate commitment, capacity, and competency to their core function - at the very least.

That was the case with one of our women's sponsorship program members, Nicole. Nicole was based in the US and her sponsor, Terri, was based in Europe. In mapping out her career roadmap, Nicole was interested in branching out to a different function within the organization. Terri was impressed by Nicole's accomplishments and her drive. So while it was a seemingly odd match on paper, Sandra took Nicole on as a protégé. To get to know how best to sponsor Nicole, Terri took the time to reach out to people in Nicole's network, ranging from her direct reports, to her peers, to her manager. She asked them about Nicole's leadership style, her competency in her role, and her potential.

Through this process, she noticed that people consistently praised Nicole for strong work ethic.

Because Terri was putting in the work to get to know Nicole and her work, she found a great match for Nicole to work on a stretch project on her team, giving her broader exposure and visibility. Those conversations gave Terri greater insight into who Nicole was as a leader and how she could help her grow into her potential - despite never meeting her in person, let alone working with her. As a sponsor, Terri was always on the lookout for great talent as part of leadership pipeline planning.

The end result is that Terri's team got to work with Nicole, allowing her to prove herself and demonstrate her capabilities.

A few months later, Nicole ecstatically accepted a new role on Terri's team and got promoted to a team lead.

This story shows that sponsorship can work even when there wasn't a strong, or established relationship beforehand. The key success factor is for the protégé to clearly articulate their capabilities and aspirations; while the sponsor committing to getting to know the protégé and their work.

Going back to the very beginning of this book we discussed the importance of defining your career North Star so your sponsor can help you position yourself to get there. A strong sponsor will help you see two or three steps ahead.

The second thing an amazing sponsor would do is to provide visibility into what's going on in the organization. In the case of Gail, who I sponsored while at SAP, I asked her to shadow me in a meeting with one of our partners at that time, Google Cloud. That gave her exposure to the kind of conversations happening in these strategic partnerships at the C-suite level.

This was the exact same access that Phil gave me when he invited me to the Mid-Year Review back when I was at Microsoft. That kind of exposure allows the protégé to absorb and learn the type of discussions at the executive level.

The next thing extraordinary sponsors would do is to champion the protégé - especially when they aren't in the room. I find this to be the most authentic and impactful benefit of sponsorship. What we've seen a lot at Tenshey is that there's still a common belief that if you train people with the right management skills, they will be equipped to grow successfully in their careers. The reality is that it may be true for some but not everyone; especially when it comes to many underrepresented minorities. The management conversations that take place behind closed doors matter. Your level of visibility matters. Because of this, sponsors are key to driving career growth by leveraging their own political capital to open doors to new opportunities. This is why we see a significant increase in promotions of women and women of color in our sponsorship programs at Tenshey. Not only are these women skilled and hard working, they now have the right level of support from the leadership team and the companies to truly reach their potential.

Underpinning all of that is a sponsor that not only believes in the protégé, but a sponsor that believes in the power of sponsorship and the role they play in cultivating the next generation of leaders.

When I look at Gail's trajectory, I started off not knowing much about her, so four years later, not only did she thrive as the CMO of a fast-growth startup, she landed her first coveted public board seat, of which I gladly obliged as her reference. Sponsor relationships may evolve but the connection tends to continue.

BECOMING AN INCLUSIVE LEADER

Like I discussed throughout this chapter, sponsorship is a true win-win-win. But it's only powerful if all parties are committed to diversity and recognize the power of sponsorship. That culminates into what it means to be an "inclusive leader".

I'm encouraged that many organizations are going beyond diversity and inclusion, with conversations elevated to include belonging and equity. The only way to do that is to foster inclusive leaders that are brave and willing to stand up for something, even when no one else does.

Inclusive leaders embody compassion and empathy for others. They seek to understand their own biases so they can address them.

In sponsorship, we talk a lot about an "allyship". To achieve gender equality, we need all hands on deck. Leaders need to be sponsors of women and other underrepresented minorities, and be an ally. Sponsor those who are rising stars in your organizations by opening your network to them, give them visibility, and advocate for them on critical projects and promotions. You don't need to be an executive to be an ally. You don't even need to be a leader to be an ally. Anyone in the organization can amplify the voice of those under-represented in meetings; say something if you feel there's micro-aggression taking place. Leaders who are willing to take action for the better good of the organization and push the envelope to build an inclusive environment are the ones that can make an impact to the organization most.

I've spoken about the lack of diversity in the tech sector. At the same time, you'll also find leaders who, despite these challenges, find a way to hire and promote diverse leaders. It just comes back down to commitment.

I still have a chuckle when I remember a Board Committee meeting with an executive recruiting firm where an executive recruiter was telling us how challenging it was to find female board of director candidates who have a technical background. Our CEO reminded them that he hired a woman of color as our Chief Information Security Officer. In other words, it can be done. You just need to dig deeper.

I also believe that inclusive leaders must commit themselves to lifelong learning. Diversity and inclusion is a complex and evolving topic. If we really want to reach those deep levels of belonging and equity, we have to let go of our own assumptions and incorporate others' opinions, their point of views.

Key Takeaways

Sponsorship is a win for all levels of the organization, assuming all parties are committed to it. Below are best practices to get the most out of it.

Best Practices for Protégés:

- **Challenge Themselves**: Challenge yourselves with a bolder vision for success by stepping out of your comfort zones.
- **Share Goals**: Share your career goals and ask for help. Sponsors can't read minds so it's up to you as the protégé to share your goals and seek advice.
- **Celebrate Success, Big and Small**: By communicating periodically of progress (your wins), you provide validation to your Sponsor that

they are betting on the right person, which enables them to consider how they may further support your career goals.

Best Practices for Sponsors:

- **Challenge the Protégé**: Challenge your protégé to a bolder vision for success they may not have dreamed of.
- **Provide Visibility**: Provide visibility and air cover that allows the Protégé to demonstrate skills and grow credibility
- **Champion the Protégé**: Champion and advocates for the protégé, especially when they are not in the room
- **Value Sponsorship**: Understand that an investment into their Protégé is also an investment into your company

8

BELONGING

"I'm *so* getting fired!"

I remember saying those words to myself as I walked back to my seat.

I was at an internal marketing summit at Microsoft back in 2010. It was early in our cloud journey and I remember the closing keynote session was given by the president of the Microsoft Office division, Stephen Elop. He was discussing the future of productivity in the workplace and how it played into Microsoft's overall cloud strategy.

It was a room full of hundreds of marketers from around the world. I eagerly listened to his speech, but I had a question at the end and I wondered whether or not I should ask it during the Q and A session.

Now, I'm not one to typically stand up in front of a microphone to ask a question. Let me rephrase, up until that point, I had *never* stood up in an event and asked a question in an open forum. I much prefer to ask my questions privately, in a one-on-one setting. At that time, I was leading the U.S. product marketing team of the first version of cloud productivity offering called BPOS and we were struggling to get the traction we needed. I felt it was my responsibility to bring up my concern and ask a question so we could better serve our company, and ultimately our customers.

The value proposition for Software as a Service (SaaS) was sound. But because the concept was so new, we were struggling with market awareness and education. Customers were hesitant to leave the traditional licensing model and switch to a cloud model. Paying a subscription fee for cloud software that you don't own vs. buying the software outright seemed... strange back then. Obviously, that's no longer the case.

Knowing that market awareness was a big challenge, I was debating whether I should ask a question about advertising. I knew that if we spent money on advertising, it would lower the sales cycle to convey our value proposition to the market. I just wasn't sure if I should ask the question in this open forum.

HARMONY VS DISRUPTION

Growing up in Hong Kong, I was raised to value harmony. It wasn't in my nature to question authority. Especially not at work. So I felt conflicted. Most people I worked with probably find it difficult to believe because I would not have a problem getting into debates with my management on marketing or go-to-market plans. But that's because I already know them and I felt at ease to share my views.

Back to the internal marketing summit, on one hand I knew that asking a question regarding advertising was to help the company and my business group, on the other hand I felt like I would be challenging one of the most senior executives in the company in an open forum and disrupting the harmony that I was raised to cultivate.

But this was bigger than me and my fears. It was about our customers and the success of the company. So just as they were asking if there were any last questions, I worked up the courage, approached the microphone, and said, "Stephen, I lead marketing for the new cloud productivity suite in the US subsidiary (which was the largest subsidiary). We're having a really hard time getting our customers to understand the product. Our distributors and channel partners are saying that the product is too hard to sell, as compared to continuing with the status quo of selling on-premise software." I went on to explain their dilemma with data. For those in the tech industry, you know how much we love data. "As an example, our partners who are selling traditional licenses could close a deal with just one email or a phone call. With BPOS, they told us that it takes four phone calls and six emails to get a deal done. It's too hard for our sellers to sell." Then I went on to make my request, "Is it possible to get some advertising in the marketplace so that we can shorten the sales cycle?"

I couldn't believe I had just asked that question to the head of the Office division in front of hundreds of my colleagues, my boss, and my boss's boss.

Steven replied "Thank you for your question. My supervisor (Steve Ballmer, then CEO of Microsoft) and I actually did talk about it. We are just not sure if the product is ready for this kind of investment yet."

In most cases, I would have just said, "Okay, thank you very much." But for some reason, I just couldn't let it go so I pressed on, "Okay Stephen, I totally get it. But maybe it's not $100 million, maybe it's not even $10 million, but we need something. If we can get something in the marketplace, that would make a huge difference," to which he said "Ok thank you. Let me think about it."

I remember walking back to my seat knowing my face was burning and feeling terrified. I sat back down in my seat next to my manager, Fred, and asked him "Do you think I'm going to get fired?"

About two weeks later, Fred got a call from the global marketing team in the Office division and they said, 'Steven has just approved $10 million for advertising BPOS in the US subsidiary.'" So Fred came to me and told me the great news. I was just ecstatic because it meant that my question meant something.

It was tough for me to step out of my comfort zone and ask the question, let alone challenge the answer that Stephen first gave me. At the same time, it wasn't about me, it was about the company and our partners and our sales team. I knew that we needed to advertise if we were ever going to make any waves, so I put my neck on the line and pushed for what I wanted.

Fast forward one year and that $10 million in investment in advertising became $100 million. The next version of the product, Office 365, went on to become one of the fastest products to reach a billion dollars in revenue in Microsoft's history.

It was such a surreal experience. I was proud of myself for tuning out my inner critic and advocate for what I felt was right for the company. Pushing authority, especially in a public forum felt so uncomfortable for me, so antithetical to my upbringing, but it was just the right thing to do.

CULTURE CLASH

I remember at the end of 2018, I was doing a keynote at the McDonald's Global Women Summit, at their brand new headquarters in downtown Chicago, my topic was "Finding your career North Star". At the end of it, an Asian woman raised her hand and said, "Maggie, I don't see a lot of Asian women in the C-suite and I want to ask you, as an Asian woman, how do you reconcile, what you feel is your culture what you need to do to advance your career?" It was a powerful question; one that resonated deep inside of me.

As mentioned, growing up in Hong Kong in traditional Chinese culture, I always strived for excellence and harmony. My family is very important to me, so that collaboration piece and team spirit was ingrained in me since childhood. In my career, it manifested itself in me seeking harmony and collaboration. For the most part, it helped me tremendously but at times, it could backfire too. The word harmony means a lot to us, meaning that we always seek "win-win" situations and avoid confrontation if possible.

It wasn't until almost 20 years later, during a corporate leadership assessment that I realized this tendency. Sometimes it manifested itself in me not taking a strong stand for my ideas. Other times it meant that I didn't speak up when I saw a better way of doing things but I didn't feel I would get enough support to proceed. No matter your culture or background, it's helpful to understand yourself and be aware of these tendencies.

As I visited other Asian countries for work, I noticed the hierarchy and deference to authority. That means that employees respect their elders and their superiors. By contrast, while American culture also values respecting authority, you're much more likely to be rewarded for challenging leadership if you have the right idea.

Being aware of my bias toward harmony and how they play out in the corporate world is really key. I've learned that when I stuck to my guns and defended my position, with evidence, it worked out well for my career, and ultimately the company. Stepping out of my comfort zone and being a bit disruptive was exactly what I needed to do.

Sometimes you have to push yourself out of your comfort zone for the greater good. It's not easy to do, but I've found that preparation and facts are the key to having the confidence to stand up for my opinions.

SPEAK UP, STAND OUT

This reminds me of when I was new at Microsoft as a senior marketing manager, I remember having a one-on-one conversation with my general manager. Eager at the chance to meet with my skip-level manager, I asked him for feedback. He responded by saying "You know Maggie, I noticed that you have really good ideas, but you don't necessarily raise them during meetings. So, one of the things I would like to see you do more is speak up in meetings."

That was great feedback and was applicable to so many other women, especially in tech where we're surrounded by men who have a tendency to get their thoughts out, very quickly I may say, in meetings. I found it hard to insert myself into the conversation and fight to get my voice heard. Sometimes, it's just exhausting!

But one of my female colleagues gave me some advice that I adopted. She told me to try to say something in the first ten minutes of a meeting - whether it's a comment, a question, or a suggestion. I thought it was excellent advice because it helped me make my voice heard early in the conversation so I wasn't worried about cutting someone off, or that someone has already said what I intended to say.

From that point forward I made sure that I added something valuable to the conversation every time I attended a meeting. Of course, you don't want to say something for the sake of saying something. As a result, it helped me hone in on my preparation for meetings.

Anytime I prepare for a meeting, whether it's a meeting I'm leading or a meeting someone else is leading, I write down the key things that I want to see the meeting accomplish. I pre-read the materials and jot down comments and questions so that I can add value to the discussion. Over time, this process has become a part of my muscle memory and has boosted my confidence and performance in discussions. I don't feel like I have to curtail what I want to say because I've done the work upfront and know that I'm adding value to the conversation.

"BEST" FIT VS "RIGHT" FIT

I was speaking to the CFO of a publicly traded tech company about their commitment to diversity and inclusion. In fact, he was the head of their Global Diversity Council and was a champion for advancing diversity at all levels of the organization.

At the same time, we were discussing hiring a candidate for a critical role and he said something that threw me for a loop. He emphasized that they needed to hire the "best" fit for the role.

Of course, everyone wants to pick the best person for the job, but I challenge leaders to rethink how they define the "best" person. I push them to broaden their lens from viewing that individual to viewing how that individual fits into the overall team. At the end of the day, we're looking to build championship teams that build championship organizations. Hiring based on an individual's pedigree, devoid of how that individual fits into the overall team is like recruiting five point guards to a basketball team and expecting it to win a championship.

Organizations, even ones dedicated to advancing diversity and inclusion have to remain intentional about building teams that represent different backgrounds, different perspectives, and all of the elements of diversity that contribute to world-class organizations.

Studies have shown that diverse teams yield better financial performance and innovation - so this isn't about hiring token employees to portray a sense of diversity - it's a competitive advantage and a business imperative. To me, this underscores the point that no matter how good your strategy is, if your culture and day-to-day practices aren't aligned, your strategy will fail.

Organizations, even sophisticated ones with formal diversity and inclusion programs, need to be careful about not thinking about "culture fit" from the paradigm of just the individual candidate because in the long run, that inadvertently subverts diversity and inclusion.

We all have unconscious bias, but we need to evolve in our thinking so we identify it and bring diversity and inclusion into play. If you look at Silicon Valley for example, for a long period of time, hiring "best" talent often translates into white males from Ivy League schools - but that excludes talent that's as good, if not better than that prototypical "best" fit.

From a diversity perspective, how do you branch out to other schools to attract a more diverse talent pool? Historically black colleges and universities are the first thing that come to mind, but there is so much more that companies could do to build a diverse leadership pipeline. Casting a wide net and recruiting from a wide range of schools and organizations builds high-performing teams that connect with the market in more meaningful ways.

I've found that focusing on building integrated, well-rounded, diverse teams helps companies build an inclusive culture that doesn't hire based on individuals, but based on how well they bring out the best in the overall team and the overall organization. The effects of that diversity cascades into financial results, breakthrough innovation, and helps with employee retention and satisfaction.

Only when there is representation (diversity), there's a chance for inclusion; and only when everyone feels that they belong, there's a chance for equality. As a result, we were able to connect with our customers better and craft messaging that resonated with the markets we served.

DEVELOPMENT AND SUPPORT

Back when I was at Microsoft, the company held a Giving Campaign in the month of October every year to emphasize giving back to the communities we serve. One of the elements of the Giving Campaign was a charitable auction where we could bid on items and experiences. I was intrigued by an auction item to shadow an executive who headed engineering for the productivity cloud business for a day.

It was a coveted experience with lots of interest. I had to find a way to win. That was when my husband told me about the auction sniping technique.

Auction sniping works in a timed online auction, of placing a bid likely to exceed the current highest bid as late as possible, usually seconds before the end of the auction, giving other bidders no time to outbid the sniper. So I waited until the last few seconds of the auction and made a bid at a price that I *knew* would guarantee that I won. I knew that the proceeds would go to charity anyway, so it was all for a good cause.

The executive's office found a day that worked for both of us. I enthusiastically went to his office on Microsoft's main campus in Redmond, Washington to shadow him for a day. I remember meeting with him in the beginning of the day so I could learn a bit about the context of the meetings I would shadow him for. The "main event" was a two-hour product review with his Engineering team, which was a fantastic experience. I gained insights into how "the sausage is made" in product development which made the entire thing so worthwhile. I then ended the day one-on-one with the executive by reflecting on what I had learned and asking him a few questions.

As much fun as the product review was, I remember sitting in a large conference room with 60 to 70 people jam packed into the room. He began that meeting by introducing me to his team and telling them that I had won the Giving Campaign auction to shadow him for the day. I remember scanning the room and noticing that it was all male. But as I looked closer, I could see at the very far corner of the room, there was a woman. I still vividly remember thinking "I wonder how she felt being in a room with all guys." as people presented their updates on the product.

Of course, I loved what I was hearing on the engineering product review, because I was on the other side of the value chain marketing the product. However, I noticed that the sole woman in the room never came up or raised her hand to speak. "Does she feel she belongs?" I wonder. I would never know. When I think about what belonging looks like, I say you need to first have representation, and you also need to ensure that everyone has a voice at the table. A sense of community is absolutely essential.

Speaking of representation, at the end of that day, I got a chance to have a one-on-one conversation with the engineering executive. It was not often that I got to speak with an executive of Asian descent, so I asked him how his culture influenced his leadership style. He shared that growing up in India, he was taught to value family and community. As a result, he worked to imbibe a sense of community and collaboration into his own team. That resonated with me. There are times I have to override what I'm accustomed to in my culture at work; other times our culture is our superpower.

"There aren't enough qualified women and minorities in the talent pool." It's a common complaint that I hear over and over again, especially in technical teams, and oftentimes it leads to all-male leadership teams. But it doesn't happen by accident. In my opinion, it happens because companies *allow* it to happen. It may not be intentional, but companies have a responsibility to come up with innovative solutions.

Businesses innovate to create products that solve a customer need. I believe that companies can apply that same ingenuity to solve the talent problem and create a more equitable workplace for all.

Women are nearly 50% of the workforce, yet they occupy a mere 25% of tech jobs. Of those 25% of women in tech, Asian women make up just 5% of that number, with Black women accounting for 3%, and Hispanic women accounting for 1%. Part of the reason is that women still trail men majoring in most STEM (Science, Technology, Engineering and Mathematics) fields in college.

The good news is companies that walk the talk in diversity and inclusion are finding ways to solve this challenge by initiating learning and development programs to cultivate that diverse population. They can pioneer entry level programs to help them create a career path to grow into leadership roles. Offering this development and support programs to women and minorities helps them feel like they belong, hence increasing retention rate of diverse talents.

THE IMPORTANCE OF ALLYSHIP

When I think about my own career journey over the past 20 plus years, 70%, if not more, of all my sponsors, and managers were male because of the nature of the business that I was in. Many of my colleagues and leaders were also male. I wouldn't get to where I am without allyship from my colleagues as part of my broader support system.

I first met Stephen through a marketing community. Not only is he an accomplished C-level executive, he exudes such warmth with anyone he interacts with. Stephen recently published his first article on LinkedIn on this very timely topic – the importance of allies. He recounted a personal story, from the earlier days in his career, when he was called in to an executive office not to celebrate one of the most successful product launches in the company's history he was leading but to speak about how he shows up, his "gayness". But his colleagues, his allies, had his back. They spoke up and rallied around him. Because of his allies, Stephen was able to see that the culture of the company was inclusive, and he continued to show up every day as his authentic self.

Stephen's story has a good outcome, but that may not be the case for all. Stephen went on to share that, according to a June 2020 report from Out Leadership, 58% of LGBTQ+ employees hide their LGBTQ+ identity from coworkers and/or supervisors. The fear of being rejected or saying something that may cause a negative response was cited as a key reason. That is why it's so important for all of us to be allies to each other. Stephen continues to share that speaking up not only helps the person experiencing any type of injustice, but also models for the people who may not yet be comfortable raising their voices to be an ally. I couldn't agree more.

Back in 2017, Sotis, my Chief of Staff at SAP asked me if we could be a sponsor at the New York City Pride Parade. As an executive sponsor for our NYC office, I asked him to share with me a proposal, and whether we would have volunteers to coordinate the efforts. There was such over-whelming support and excitement from the local employ-ees, we went ahead with the plan. During the NYC Pride March, which was my first, not only did we have a strong showing of our LGBTQ+ employees and allies, many leaders from our neighboring States also came in for support.

The surprising part for me was the emails I have received from our employees across the country. The stories they shared and what it meant to them to have allies was what I remember most.

PAYING IT FORWARD

As I rose through my career, I made it a point to advance gender and racial diversity and to build a diverse and inclusive leadership pipeline. The same goes to many executives I know who have had sponsors who opened doors to opportunities for them.

As you engage and benefit from sponsorship, you have immense power to pay it forward to the next generation of leaders. You can be the proverbial pebble in the pond to affect change. Don't underestimate the power you have to make a difference.

Earlier in this book, I mentioned the concept of leading without authority and described it as leading even when you don't have an official leadership role by acting as a leader. That includes sharing best practices with colleagues, mentoring others, providing feedback, etc. Those actions will help you stand out and show that you're willing to build up your team and help the broader organization achieve its goals.

Here are some of the things that you can do to pay it forward to the next generation.

1). Lead an Employee Resource Group: You could create or join an affinity group within your organization, commonly known as an Employee Resource Group (ERG). You could play an active role in establishing and leading a Asian ERG, Black ERG, a Pride ERG, a Woman ERG, Next Gen ERG, and etc.

2). Mentor Others: You could officially mentor and sponsor others within the organization. If your company doesn't have an official sponsorship or mentorship program, you could propose one. Doing so informally is also a way to go.

3). Youth Outreach: You could help the younger generation who are in college, high school, or even elementary school. If you're in tech, reaching out to younger kids is an amazing way to get them interested in STEM early and visualize a career in technology. If you remember the story of Lisa from earlier in this book, she told me about how she volunteers to teach kids on cyber-safety, to protect themselves online. She's paying it forward to the younger generation by getting them interested in technology and keeping away from the bad actors.

As you rise through the ranks of the organization you can be an agent of change and create a sense of inclusion and belonging for the next generation. This comes back to the concept of leading without authority and proves that you don't need to be an executive to start paying it forward.

Key Takeaways

- **Stand Up for What You Believe In**: One of the strongest things you can do is to advocate for others. Taking a stand for your team, your partners, and your customers gives you the strength and confidence to push for your ideas.
- **Know Yourself**: Knowing your background, your culture and how it shapes your perceptions will help you leverage them for strengths and tune out your inner critic.
- **Redefine "Fit"**: Companies need to redefine what they mean when they're looking for the "best" fit. If you're looking for a new role, learn to position yourself as a valuable addition to the team, not

because of your "sameness", but because of your uniqueness.

- **Build Allies**: Always build allies within your organization. Your allies will likely be your peers, colleagues and leaders in the organization. Having a strong ally network enhances your sense of belonging.

- **Pay It Forward**: Don't underestimate your power to create a more inclusive organization, no matter how new you are or the level you're at in an organization. You can create or lead an employee resource group, recruit on college campuses, or volunteer at high schools and elementary schools.

9

LEADERSHIP

We've spent a lot of time in this book discussing the power of sponsorship and its numerous benefits to protégés, sponsors, AND organizations; and what you as an individual can do to seize the opportunity to grow your careers. I've seen its transformational power in my own personal career, and I've seen it advance gender and ethnic diversity within companies, building out robust leadership pipelines that embody their values of equity and inclusion.

At the same time, I would be remiss if I didn't discuss what organizations as a whole can do to bolster this trend, because if we're going to see the equity and inclusion numbers that we all want to see, there needs to be a commitment at the macro level. That even goes as high up as at the government level, down to organizations, departments, and individual teams.

There's a large body of research showing that diversity makes business sense. Companies that promote sponsorship in their work culture add more value, innovation, and help the next generation of leaders. While there has been an increased focus on diversity in leadership, there are also setbacks. In the U.S. for example, 80% of those who left the workforce during the COVID-19 Pandemic were women. Even before the pandemic, women were doing the majority of work at home and as caregivers. The pandemic caused schools and childcare centers to close which added even more work for parents, especially women. Many organizations don't have policies to support women who are doing the majority of work and caregiving at home, which makes it harder for women to balance professional and personal lives.

ALL HANDS ON DECK

In 2021, The World Economic Forum predicted that it will now take 135.6 years to reach gender equality; a delay of 36 years due to COVID-19 Pandemic, so our work is cut out for us.

To reverse the trend, both the private and the public sector can set goals for diversity, as well as creating the infrastructure for child & elderly care so more women can stay in the workforce. As an example, the United Kingdom set a minimum target requiring 33% of board of directors to be women, and at least one ethnic minority in the largest public companies in the FTSE 350.

In December of 2020, NASDAQ put a stick in the ground and proposed listing rules that would require all companies listed on the NASDAQ to publish diversity statistics regarding their board of directors. The rules stated that all companies on the exchange would need to have, or explain why they don't have, at least two diverse directors, including one who self-identifies as female and one who self-identifies as either an underrepresented minority or LGBTQ+. Their rationale for the decision was a detailed analysis of over two dozen studies that found a link between diverse boards and better financial performance and more robust corporate governance. This move proves once again how important diversity and inclusion is not only to the overall culture, but to business performance.

In the United States, since California passed the board diversity law in 2018 mandating that public companies headquartered in the state have at least one woman on their boards of directors by the end of 2019, the percentage of California-based public companies with all-male boards has dropped from 30% to 3%, with a 66.5% increase in the number of board seats held by women. To continue its push for increased diversity on corporate boards, California Governor signed into law a bill that requires publicly held companies headquartered in the state to include board members from underrepresented communities in 2020.

These moves are game changers because the board of directors is the governing body for the entire company. It's where the CEO reports into. It sets the direction for the entire company. A diverse board can help see around blind spots and offer insights that less diverse boards can't.

In the private sector, more and more companies are publishing their diversity numbers and goals, not only shining a light on the issue, but tracking the actions and subsequent results. These are all good steps that build momentum on the path toward gender diversity.

To achieve gender equality, we need all hands on deck. Leaders need to be sponsors and allies of women and minorities. I implore leaders to sponsor women who are rising stars in your organizations by opening your network to them, giving them visibility, and advocating for them on critical projects and promotions. And for everyone, and I do mean everyone, be an ally. You can amplify the voices of those underrepresented in meetings and speak up if you feel there's microaggression. That's the power you have in you.

CAN YOU MEASURE IT?

World-renowned management guru Peter Drucker famously said, "What gets measured gets managed" and I can tell you from my experience in the tech industry, no one measures, analyzes, computes, and quantifies better than tech companies. The tech industry is obsessed in interpreting data, deriving insights, and taking action based on that data.

Given that DEI is a business imperative, we need to treat it as such. That means we should have data, we should have goals, and we should have measurable initiatives that support those goals. In my work at Tenshey and on boards, I'm starting to see companies include their DEI goals in their ESG (Environmental, Social, and Governance) reports or in their diversity and inclusion reports. Institutional investors are increasingly applying these non-financial factors as part of their analyses to assess growth opportunities and risks. This is especially important for public companies. It is not a coincidence that we are seeing more ESG committees being formed on public boards.

Russell Reynolds Associates released a report citing a survey of C-level executives at companies with $1 billion or more in revenue tied compensation to the achievement of corporate goals. On average, 47% of British companies tied executive compensation to DEI and ESG metrics compared to 21% of US companies that tied executive compensation to DEI. US companies have been making advances, but nowhere near the pace of British companies. The intent isn't to castigate companies, rather the goal is to have an awareness of the current state.

As companies embark on DEI initiatives, the data may reveal the lack of diversity in the organization, and that's ok. In the early days, it's merely a starting data point that provided insight into the current state of affairs, and got the discussions started to create visibility and awareness. Creating a baseline of diversity data in the organization is a first step to create an action plan to foster a diverse and inclusive culture.

Once you have an awareness, you can galvanize the entire organization on the importance of diversity and inclusion, how DEI goals are set to meet the challenge and give each leader the steps they need to take to achieve them.

As an example, when I first joined SAP in 2014, it had already set a three-year target for gender diversity. At the time, the company had established a goal to have 25% of leadership to be women by 2017 and shared publicly. The fact that we had a goal gave us something to strive for. So before we hit the target date in 2017, we had already reached that goal and were setting the next three year target. That's how we created not only awareness, but momentum around it. It created a culture where managers and leaders were held accountable to hitting those goals.

LOWERING THE BAR?

Setting goals for diversity has its fair share of controversy. There has been pushback that setting diversity goals would mean "lower the bar" for talents, or that it is a bias against white males. Some underrepresented minorities feel it jeopardizes their chances to earn their seat by merits versus being a diversity token. My view is that by setting diversity goals, organizations signal to their employees, customers, investors and other stakeholders that they are taking DEI seriously and are putting accountability on themselves. In my experience, organizations and leaders at large are quite thoughtful in how they combine short- and longer-term plans to meet the challenge. Having a goal as a guidepost is simply a way to monitor progress, similar to how we use KPIs (Key Performance Indicators) to measure business progress.

The tide is already turning towards a more diverse and inclusive workplace. In the war for talent, you don't want to stand out for the wrong reasons. I am by no means saying that setting diversity goals is the only solution, but it is a viable one that has produced results in this complex challenge.

The second piece of a sound DEI strategy is creating hiring and promotion policies that support an inclusive workplace. One thing we witnessed during the COVID-19 pandemic was that the burden of childcare and elderly care still falls primarily on women. The question becomes, what are organizations doing to support parents so that they can better fulfill their professional and personal responsibilities. Balancing that is important to keeping women in the workforce.

Policies that support not only women, but also men that want to spend more time with their families are important for organizations to think deliberately about. As baby boomers age and retire, caring for them will create an enormous social and economic strain not only on individual families, but on the economy as a whole. Smart corporations are paying attention to these trends and planning for them.

As a board director, and a fierce advocate for diversity in leadership, one of the things I look at is whether an organization has a protocol to measure their progress. Are they regularly collecting DEI data and digging into the numbers to paint a picture of the state of affairs? As an example, it's not uncommon for an organization to report an increase in the percentage of women in leadership, but if you peel the onion and look across the different functions, that reveals a very telling story. What I see, especially in tech, is that we see a higher percentage of women in HR and marketing. Those are functions that traditionally have more women and that's great, but when it comes to line management, or technical roles, there's still very much an uphill battle.

It's a pervasive problem based on how women and girls view themselves vis a vis science and engineering roles. Edutopia.org cited a study where children were asked to draw pictures of a mathematician or scientist. Boys almost universally drew men in a lab coat, but girls were twice as likely to draw pictures of men portraying these roles as they were to draw women. These perceptions start early and carry-on over decades. I believe it's one of the many contributing factors to why more women aren't in technical roles in organizations. The most interesting piece of research from the article was that girls perform as good at math as boys. In elementary school, girls perform on par, or better than boys, with girls passing middle school algebra at higher rates than boys. The disparity in performance is virtually non-existent in high school as well. But problems start to emerge after high school, with race and class impacting the educational decisions young women make in college.

That's why I believe all levels of society have a responsibility in creating policies that work to correct these gender disparities. And it starts with measuring where you are and creating initiatives to rectify the situation.

THE DEFINITION OF INSANITY

Albert Einstein famously said "Insanity is doing the same thing over and over and expecting different results".

In my practice at Tenshey, I speak to some organizations that may have aspirations to become more diverse and inclusive, but aren't moving the needle in a positive direction. There are a few common factors I have seen to be the causes. This lack of progress usually stems from some broader challenges in a combination of the absence of CEO-level support, lack of empowerment to those responsible for DEI strategy, and/or lack of measurable accountability.

If you're tracking your DEI data for a few quarters, or even a few years, and aren't seeing any improvement, it may be time to examine what's getting in the way of you making progress so you can take corrective action.

We speak to a lot of organizations that have great DEI goals, which is fantastic. In fact, they're making changes and seeing positive results, but it may only apply to the top of the organization through external recruitment. There may be more females and minorities in the C-suite or the VP level, but that diversity isn't reflected when you look across the entire organization.

Part of the reason for this disconnect is that while they're setting their goals at the top, there's no accountability across the different levels of management. Like any endeavor, when you don't put accountability on leaders, it's not likely that they'll take impactful action. That's why some organizations have great momentum at the top levels, but not across the board. Because we work with so many organizations, the consistent challenge we see with those companies that aren't making meaningful progress in DEI is that lack of accountability.

The other thing we see in companies that we've talked to is that they may have robust mentorship programs, but mentorship alone doesn't create the environment of accountability to help diverse talents get the visibility, advocacy, and collaboration they need for them to accelerate within the organization. That's not to say that organizations shouldn't have mentorship programs. Mentorship is a critical component to build a skill set for individuals. But without the sponsorship, it's not likely that high-performing talent will get the exposure they need and deserve to advance into leadership and further their careers.

While I have witnessed many organizations and leaders passionately champion DEI within their organizations and their industry, I have also heard of horror stories. Janet, an engineering leader in a mid-sized technology company, reached out to us at Tenshey interested in our women sponsorship programs and executive coaching. As an Asian American woman and one of very few ethnic minority leaders in the company, she thought she could champion change. She worked with our team to ensure she gets familiar with the programs and asked lots of questions to anticipate any objection handling. She really tried. Months later, after multiple tries, with different executives and functions, she told us that she tried everything, and it wasn't going to work. I heard the story from my team and suggested that I offer Janet a mentoring session, if she chooses to. She quickly accepted.

When we spoke, Janet shared a story of an HR executive within her company suggesting she should get mentored by Jim, an Asian American executive, because Jim found a way to "fit in". "RUN!" that's the voice in my head. Through the stories Janet told me, it was evident that Diversity and Inclusion was a nice-to-have, not a must-have priority at the company. The effort was delegated to the HR function. Of course, the HR function is typically the Go-To function for strategizing and implementing DEI initiatives. But what I have seen time and time again is that if Diversity and Inclusion isn't a business imperative championed by the CEO, it rarely gets the broad support of other business unit leaders to make the impact desired. And at the end, it will be the company that loses out on retaining great talents. In the case of Janet, she was already building her exit plan from the company.

Rather than looking at sponsorship and DEI as a chore, it comes down to reframing how the organization views it. When you look at DEI as a business imperative, embarking on sponsorship becomes a win for the organization. When you look at it through that angle, it's a lot easier to build internal momentum and align your actions with that vision.

CELEBRATE SUCCESS

One of the really heart-warming things about starting Tenshey is seeing the impact that we can make for not only individuals, but for the organizations as well. I want organizations to be able to see that when executives become sponsors, they open themselves up to new experiences. Oftentimes, they build compassion and empathy in the process.

I say that because when an executive sponsors a woman, or a person of color, or someone who is LGBTQ+, or any other underrepresented minority, you're exposed to experiences from the lens of someone else's eyes. In fact, when you see how they utilize their skills, and how they execute on their competencies, you gain insight into how they tackle challenges. And I've heard many examples where the sponsors gained tremendous insights on the changing business operations and customer feedback on the ground from their protégé because they are a lot closer to the frontline. This insight makes you a better leader, and ultimately a better communicator because you can relate to different experiences and perceptions.

Not only that, if you can help your protégés by pushing them to expand their competencies, or help them gain visibility and expand their network, you can take pride in the role you played in their success. It's really a great feeling to see someone rise through the ranks and make a huge impact on the organization, knowing that you played a part in that.

Practicing what we preach, we at Tenshey always gather data and insights from our corporate clients during our sponsorship engagements where we speak directly with the individual sponsors and one of the questions we ask is "How do you celebrate success with your protégé, small or large?" A small success could be a connection that you made that helps the protégé gain new insights into a new role. Or maybe it's something bigger like helping them with a promotion.

Funny enough, an overwhelming majority of our sponsors don't have an answer. They may acknowledge the win, but they quickly move on to the next task at hand. This isn't atypical, given the fast-paced nature of their business, but I also think that there's real value in taking a moment to pause and really celebrate those successes. The reason it's so important is that we hear people tell us how impactful sponsorship has been in their career. We have people tell us "I'm not the same person that I was 8 months ago [before the sponsorship program]!" because of the confidence they now have in themselves and the opportunities that they're exposed to. They're more assertive at work, they take on stretch projects, and they feel like they're acknowledged. As a result, they see a clear path forward and take on more risks and responsibility as they chart the next phase of their career. They've built the "muscles" to identify sponsors, add value to them, and make an impact on their careers - and these are skills that they can take with them throughout their careers.

For organizations, they see how well sponsorship works and embody it into their culture so that leaders understand how they aren't only sponsoring high-potential talent, but how they are intentionally expanding opportunities to diverse talent that they may have not considered before. Doing that builds a more inclusive culture, increasing the sense of engagement and belonging that employees feel.

That's why celebrating success is so important; it reinforces that good that you're doing and the results that you're generating. It's not intuitive, and it may even feel awkward at first, but it's a key part of reinforcing that culture of inclusion. I can say that from my personal experience. I've been trained throughout my life and my career to always strive for "what's next". Mary, my coach, is often the person who would point out the significance of milestones I have achieved, big and small. She would say, "Maggie, this is huge, let's take a moment to talk about it and celebrate." I notice how it energizes me and that's why I'm intentional about doing it for others now. So I completely understand it is a skill that needs to be learned and exercised repeatedly. I'm becoming more intentional about this myself, especially when I'm sponsoring someone or working with people on my team. I remind them of the milestones that they've achieved and how significant they are. From their facial expression over our computer screens, I would see that sometimes they were amazed by their own learnings and achievements. Even if it's just an email acknowledging their achievement, it's good to put it in context and celebrate it.

Key Takeaways

- **The DEI Imperative:** Organizations throughout the country are paying attention to the business impact of DEI and are being measured by it
- **All Hands on Deck:** Since DEI is such an important initiative, all levels of society from governments, to the media, to the education system, to corporate executives, to front line managers, need to do their share in building a more diverse, equitable, and inclusive workplace.
- **Celebrate Success:** The path to DEI is a long journey, so celebrate successes along the way. Celebrate your organizational successes, team successes, or individual successes, big and small.

CONCLUSION

In corporate America, only 21% of executive level managers are women, and only four percent are women of color. We've come a long way in equality, but we still have work to do especially in today's business environment.

Companies that incorporate sponsors in their work culture add more value, innovation, and help the next generation of leaders.

I saw firsthand how male-dominated the workforce was in the tech industry, specifically in executive-level positions. I made it my mission to foster equality and inclusion in the workplace by empowering leaders of all backgrounds.

I created Tenshey to do just that. We believe in paying it forward and helping the next generation of talent become successful leaders. I've dedicated my life to empowering leaders of all backgrounds through executive and career coaching.

I have written this book to share the steps I took to break through the glass ceiling and achieve my dream career.

I hope you enjoyed it.

THE SPONSORSHIP CHEAT SHEET

EARLY CAREER

- **Explore Opportunities**: Don't be afraid to explore different jobs early in your career. There is no wrong choice.
- **Know Yourself**: Your career path isn't linear. Moving into different roles allows you to figure out what you enjoy and clarify your Career North Star.
- **One Lead Focus at a Time**: Be intentional about focusing on your professional aspirations, your financial goals, and your purpose. Be clear on all three, keep one lead focus at a time
- **Align Your Goals to Your Sponsor**: Align your goals with chain of command and your sponsor(s). If you help them achieve their goals, they'll more likely to help advance your career
- **Take On Stretch Projects**: Differentiate yourself by taking on stretch projects (when you can) which can help you level up your skills
- **Tune Out the Inner Noise**: Don't be your own

worst critic. Learn to silence the inner voice that tells you that you aren't good enough

MID-CAREER

- **Map out Your Career Roadmap**: It gives you a directional focus on where you want to take your career and enable you to take intentional steps to reach your career North Star
- **Craft Your Value Proposition**: Craft your value proposition as you prepare for new jobs and to climb the corporate ladder. This helps others to know how you can add value to the team
- **Speak Up in the First Ten Minutes**: If you have a problem getting your voice heard in meetings, make it a goal to speak up in the first ten minutes. Your preparation will help you add value to the conversation
- **Get multiple sponsors**: You don't need to find sponsors who look like you. Your sponsors are your leaders who will advocate for you, and open doors to new opportunities
- **Think Two Jobs Ahead**: As you are ready for your new job, don't just think about your next role, but the "next-next" role.
- **A Coach Is Your Secret Weapon**: Hiring a coach can help you accelerate your leadership growth and hold you accountable to your career goals. Many companies will subsidize the cost
- **Embrace Adversity, Failure, and Setbacks**: Failure, mistakes, and setbacks are part of your career journey. Every executive has their share of stories. There are massive learnings in these experiences

- **Build Your Support System**: Your support system will help you push through the hardship and cheer your success

LEADERSHIP LEVEL

- **Pay It Forward**: Now that you're in leadership, pay it forward by sponsoring others. It will build a leadership pipeline and enhance your leadership brand as you continue to advance your career
- **Foster a Sense of Belonging**: It's now your responsibility to foster a sense of belonging among your team and broader organization
- **Celebrate Your Teams' Success**: You have the power to transform and inspire. Use it by celebrating when your team does something noteworthy
- **Treat DEI as a Competitive Edge**: DEI is a competitive advantage. More companies are being measured by it so keep it as a front focus
- **Be an Ally**: While anyone can be an ally, especially to those whose voices are marginalized. As a leader, you set an example for others in the organization

ACKNOWLEDGMENTS

To make writing this book possible, I have a lot of people to thank.

First and foremost, I've had nineteen managers in my twenty-year career in corporate America. I have deep gratitude to my managers, mentors, and sponsors. Thanks to them, I got to enjoy a fulfilling career that allowed me to pay it forward, and to share the stories and lessons in this book.

More specifically, I want to start by thanking Peter Hews and Peter Van Oppen. Not only were they the first people to give me the opportunities at ADIC when I started my career in the tech industry, but also shared valuable insights for this book.

I want to thank my manager Marcia Kennedy at Sun Microsystems who was the first manager to tell me that I have a long runway ahead of me in my career. I didn't know what she meant when she said it, but looking back now, I can see what she was referring to, and I often borrow that phrase when speaking with high potential next generation leaders. Souheil Saliba and Laura Finkelstein gave me my first opportunity to lead a flagship product line and launch at Sun. Diane Lee and Annie Lin Johnson were my early mentors at Sun who also happened to be Asian American women. Representation matters. It was wonderful to get to learn from them.

At Microsoft, I had many managers, mentors, and sponsors, and I know I won't be able to name all of them. Allison Watson, Gavriella Schuster, Jon Roskill, Phil Sorgen, Fred Studer, Marie Huwe, Dan Fennell, Gretchen O'Hara, Angus Norton, Jane Boulware, and many others have made a long-lasting impact in my career journey.

At Level 3, I got to witness and learned from an inclusive executive team in action, starting from the CEO, Jeff Storey and CHRO at the time, Laurinda Pang, my manager Andrew Crouch who was the President of North America, Global CMO Anthony Christie, and Sunit Patel, CFO. It was amazing to be part of the broader executive team in driving Level 3's business transformation.

And then of course, at SAP, thanks to Bill McDermott, who gave me the opportunity to realize my career "North Star" to become a Global CMO and Stefan Ries, CHRO who had been an ally, and continues to be a great friend.

To all the team and team members I have had the privilege to lead, without them, the accomplishments would not have been achievable. Their leadership journey and growth were what inspired me to pursue my passion through the founding of my company Tenshey.

I also want to thank the people who have shared their stories with me in this book. Without their stories, this book would have missed some of the valuable insights and experiences that they bring to the table; Asha George, Brian

Reaves, Gail Moody-Byrd, Jade Kwok, Lisa Riviere and many others we are fortunate to work with at Tenshey.

And my team at Tenshey; I want to thank Haley Milano and Ali Ongvorapong, and our intern Nell Curtin. They have been a tremendous support not only in writing this book, but in helping me to read, re-read, and launching this book. And a big thanks to Raza Imam, my writing partner, Ginny Musante Erickson who kick started the initial writing with me, and Judy Klym, my media specialist, for making this book possible.

Last but not least, and most importantly, the support of my family JP Jones and Charlie is unwavering. As I wrote the majority of this book during the COVID-19 Pandemic, Charlie was by my side every step of the way.

Finally, I would also say that I personally had never imagined myself to be an author, publishing my own book. To the people who know me, my writing style is concise and to the point, and usually in bullet points format. To see this book coming to life, it is unbelievable. I always believe that where there's a will, there's a way. So, keep on living big dreams and know that sometimes dreams take longer than expected to mature. But if you keep the passion and keep the focus, anything is possible.

Made in the USA
Middletown, DE
11 October 2022